CONNECTING WITH HINDU INTERNATIONAL STUDENTS

SHARING THE GOOD NEWS
WITH CULTURAL WISDOM

W. STEPHENS

•

Published by InterVarsity International Student Ministry.
Printed in the USA.

ISBN 978-0-9978105-0-9
Some names in this booklet have been changed
to protect the individuals' privacy.

CONTENTS

FOREWORD

We live at an incredible moment in world history and for the Great Commission. People from everywhere are everywhere. Your doctor, neighbor, or co-worker may have been born on the other side of the world. A friend of mine recently completed his Ph.D. in cutting-edge electrical engineering research. At the same time his isolated village in India received electricity for the first time. People who were once *geographically distant* from hearing the good news of Christ are now in our neighborhoods and universities. However, many remain *culturally distant* from the gospel. They come from cultural groups with minimal gospel witness. This is especially true for the South Asian world where the proportion of genuine disciples of Jesus remains small compared to the overall population. Even now living in close proximity to Bible-believing churches or sitting beside Christian co-workers, many have not had significant encounters with genuine believers. The gospel remains a mystery, clouded by stereotypes and misunderstandings. But it doesn't have to stay that way.

The purpose of this booklet is to encourage you to lovingly connect with the South Asians that God puts in your world. They are a delightful and fascinating cultural group who may even embarrass you by their hospitality. It doesn't need to be complicated, and you don't need to become an expert. A willingness to love, learn, and even make mistakes will go a long way. As you share your life authentically there will be  many opportunities to show what Christ has done. But you may encounter misunderstandings and cultural differences along the way. This booklet aims to help you navigate these. It doesn't intend to be comprehensive but to provide a helpful point of orientation. You will learn about a fascinating part of the world and perhaps be one of the first believers that a South Asian Hindu or Muslim has really known personally.

South Asia denotes a broad, culturally similar region of the Indian subcontinent. Politically, South Asia includes India, Sri Lanka, Nepal,

Pakistan, and Bangladesh. This diverse region often shares common cultural elements such as food, languages, and history. Thus, a basic familiarity with shared South Asian cultural elements will apply beyond the Hindu world. The practices of the region's Christians, Sikhs, Buddhists, and Muslims have also been influenced by the culture. In fact, simply sharing a cup of *chai* (tea) and *chaat* (salty snacks) with a South Asian Muslim is probably a better place to start than learning answers to religious objections.

Religiously, the focus of this booklet is on those with a Hindu heritage. The aim is not to give an exhaustive understanding of Hindu religion. That depth is not needed to get started, and the diversity of Hinduism makes that a challenge even for scholars. This booklet does aim to show some big picture aspects of Hinduism and set them alongside similar or more familiar concepts from the Bible. Further, many of these concepts will overlap other South Asian religions including Buddhism, Jainism, and Sikhism. The intent is to help you connect well without being intimidated by the unfamiliarity of these cultural and religious backgrounds.

Most specifically, this booklet focuses on Hindu international students from India, although South Asia is sometimes used somewhat interchangeably. India is the primary focus for several reasons. For one, India ranks second behind China as the most populous nation of the world and will likely surpass it in a few years. Its growing economy and links with the U.S. technology industry provide an ongoing stream of students, workers, and professionals in many industries. Behind China, India has ranked numerically as the second highest country of origin for international students in the U.S. for the past ten to twenty years with currently over 150,000 students. A visit to the graduate engineering or computer science programs of many university campuses in the U.S. will illustrate this. Most of my personal experience is with Indian international students—first as a graduate engineering student and later as a campus ministry worker and during many trips to India.

Finally, while considering the challenges of the past this booklet is intentionally forward-looking. It focuses on the *younger generation* of Indian international students, recognizing the changing cultural landscape of South Asia. However, much of it will apply more broadly to neighbors or co-workers from South Asia regardless of age or background.

My prayer for this booklet is that it would help you to "get" your South Asian friends and avoid misunderstandings that impair genuine and clear communication—that is, to understand some of their heritage and how that impacts what they think about God/gods, what they think of Christians and Christianity, what they value, and how to genuinely connect relationally and spiritually. That way, you will have a better idea of where their objections come from and what Scriptures and themes resonate with them. You will find that the Bible may share more in common culturally with the Hindu world than it does the secular Western world (such as arranged marriages, temple worship, family structure, and spiritual outlook).

Ultimately, my prayer is that the gospel would be heard as good news of the living and loving God who came to restore people from all nations into fellowship with him.

In 2008, Anand Mahadevan, an editor of the Indian news magazine *Outlook Business*, published a one-page story of his journey to faith in Christ from a Hindu family. The article was provocatively entitled "I, the Convert" in light of the social and political tensions present in India over the issue of conversion. It concisely addresses many stereotypes and misunderstandings of how "becoming a Christian" is perceived in the diverse world of India. Most of these are well known by those from South Asia (Christian believers and non-believers alike) but less so by those outside that region. It shows that being Hindu is as much a cultural identity as it is a religious one. And it shows the impact that a genuine Christian friend had in Anand's life. His story serves as an excellent example with which to begin.

I, The Convert
My conversion was not a change of religion, it was a change of heart.
OPINION BY ANAND MAHADEVAN

I was born a Brahmin and am the grandson of a priest whom I dearly loved. I am educated and my current professional standing indicates that I am reasonably intelligent. I am also affluent and my income would put me distinctly in the upper middle class bracket. I guess that would make me high-caste, rich and smart. In other words, I am not a tribal, or poor or dim-witted. And yet, I chose to become a follower of Jesus Christ.

The world would call me a convert to Christianity. I have no problems with that, though I see my faith more as a relationship with God through Jesus Christ than as a religion. And for the record, I can truthfully claim that no one financially induced or threatened or deceived me into converting to Christianity.

I am fiercely proud of my national identity as an Indian and I am completely at peace with my cultural identity as a Hindu. I retain the name my parents gave me. My wife, who also shares my faith, continues to go by her Hindu name. We have two children and we have given both distinctly Hindu names. In fact, many of my colleagues and acquaintances who may happen to read this column are likely to be surprised. They have no inkling about my faith, for I generally don't go about announcing it. But if someone does ask me the reason behind the joy and hope that is ever present in my life, I am always delighted to share it with them.

I write this piece to make one point—that my conversion was not a change of religion but a change of heart. To explain this, I need to go back to my childhood in Chennai, similar to that of so many other Tamil Brahmin boys like me. My grandfather, every bit the virtuous priest, had enormous influence over me. I absolutely adored him and as a toddler, always clung to him. He too loved me to a fault. There was no wish of mine that he would not rush to fulfill. But even in my early, formative years I was unable to relate to the religion he fervently practiced. Later, in my school days, I once spent my summer holidays with him in Trichy. Memories of dawn walks with him, for the ritualistic dip in the Cauvery river, cow in tow, are still fresh in my memory. I learnt many shlokas, some of which I still remember. But I never understood any of it and none of it helped me connect with God.

When I was 19, a Christian friend with whom I used to play cricket invited me to his house for prayer. If he had invited me to a pub, or party, I would have gone too. At his home, he and his sister prayed for me. It was a simple yet delightful conversation with God that lasted all of five minutes. I don't remember it verbatim, but they articulated a prayer of blessing on my life, future, career and family. It was a simple affair—no miracles, no angels visitting. All they did was utter a deep human cry out to the creator God and His only son Jesus Christ. When they said Amen, I felt in my heart a desire to follow Jesus.

It was a faith encounter with God that I shall not even attempt to understand, rationalize or explain. I simply accept it. It is my faith. It is what I choose to believe. That evening I did not change my religion, for in reality I had none. Hinduism was my identity, not my religion. It still is.

The Christianity I acquired that evening is not a religion. On the contrary, it is an intensely intimate relationship with Jesus. Over the past fifteen years, I have come to know this Jesus even closer. I know Him as the pure and sinless Son of a Holy God. And I know Him as a

dear friend to whom I pray and talk to every day—about my career, my dreams, successes, failures, finances and even my sexuality. If I read a good book, watch a good movie (*Rock On* is terrific, mate), or eat a good meal at a new restaurant, I would naturally tell my friends about it. In Jesus, I have discovered a truly amazing friend, guide, leader, saviour and God. How can I not tell all my friends about Him? And if anyone does listen and he too comes to believe in Jesus, I am delighted. The world would call it a conversion; I call it a change of heart, like mine.

But I would never force anyone to listen to me, leave alone financially induce, coerce or con him into believing. That to me is pointless and against the very grain of my faith. But I do have a constitutional right to practice my faith and to preach it without deception, force or bribery. It pains to see such basic rights of mankind being cruelly violated every day in this great Hindu nation. God bless India.[1]

Did anything in this story surprise you? Anand's brief testimony introduces many South Asian cultural elements and stereotypes. Reading between the lines, you can see how he addresses false perceptions about the Christian faith and relevant elements in his experience. To begin exploring how to connect meaningfully with Hindu students, we will look briefly at India's diversity and the family's role in shaping cultural identity.

▶ DIVERSITY: "WE ARE ALL MINORITIES IN INDIA"

"Mera Bharat mahan" (My India is great) is a patriotic slogan you will see plastered on the backs of buses and trucks throughout India. It is indeed a great country—population, diversity, history, etc. Indians like Anand are rightfully proud of their ancient shared heritage. But it is an incredibly diverse country—perhaps more like a collection of countries. Consider the following:

NATIONALLY India is the second most populous nation in the world and likely to become the most populous country in a few decades. It is the world's largest democracy with more than a dozen national political parties.

ETHNICALLY India currently has 29 states with 22 official languages and over 1,000 dialects. Caste divisions further stratify ethnic groups even among those with a common language.

RELIGIOUSLY The majority of Indians are Hindu, numbering around 800 million. India is arguably the second-largest Muslim country in the world. Buddhism began in India, and Christianity, which is only a small fraction of the population (2-4%), has groups which trace their history to the beginning of the Christian era.

SOCIO-ECONOMICALLY India has perhaps one-third of the world's global poor. Yet there is a vast emerging middle class and the country is home to some of the world's wealthiest individuals.

It is important to note the depth and impact of this diversity. It is not just that there are many languages and ethnic groups, rich and poor, elite and uneducated in the same country. That is true almost everywhere in the world. Rather, there are so many diverse communities living side by side that everyone identifies with their small community. A well-known Indian author, Shashi Tharoor concludes that "we are all minorities in India."[2]

That is a significant observation. There is a sense of national unity and patriotism. But Indian society is not homogeneous. Tharoor goes on to say, "If America is a melting pot, then to me India is a Thali, a selection of sumptuous dishes in different bowls. Each tastes different, and does not necessarily mix with the next, but they belong together on the same plate..."[3] It is a country of minorities, groups and sub-groups struggling either for survival for those at the bottom or

Thali - photo by SwatiGupta1986
tiny.cc/thali86

for upward mobility for those with some means. Thus, the competition for resources and the diversity of cultures mean that your identity and welfare are linked with your family and extended family.

Family is central—in contrast to the individualistic and often isolated world of America. P. K. Varma, who writes about the Indian middle class, says "Isolation threatens Indians. Their conditioning from birth is to belong to a group: caste, kin or extended family."[4] That is because India is simply not a society that is convenient for individual living. Tharoor says the same thing, noting that "to get anything done in India we require other people—allies who see their interest as ours. Such allies are most readily found within the cocoon of the family unit."[5]

You can probably imagine that a person's family and cultural identity would be closely tied to their religion. Indeed, religion is determined not by personal, individual choice but by the community and family in which you were born. Therefore, a *change of religion is no small matter and is seen as a change of cultural identity with repercussions for your family and extended family.* In fact, "conversion" is perceived primarily to be a change in cultural communities rather than a spiritual matter.

▶ CULTURAL ADDRESS

Given this diversity, everyone in India has a *cultural address* which defines something of their origin and location in society. Did you notice this in Anand's story? In the first line, he locates himself within the diverse cultural world of India and unpacks more of that throughout the story. If you are unfamiliar with Indian geography, it would help to know that Tamil refers to a South Indian language spoken in the state of Tamil Nadu, and Brahmin refers to Anand's family's priestly caste (the highest within Hinduism). Most Indians would know this information simply from his name. In other words, he gave his cultural address which identifies his family birth community. He further described his priestly family line and his grandfather's religious devotion in the historic city of Trichy. So, he leaves no doubt to his family of origin and his deep love for them and appreciation of his Hindu culture.

▶ DOES "HINDU" IDENTIFY A RELIGION OR CULTURE?

If a Hindu like Anand chooses to follow Christ, does that change his *cultural address* within this diverse framework of India? Does he now belong to a "Christian" culture even though he speaks a different language from those in the Catholic neighborhood in his city or the Orthodox church in the neighboring state? Or is he still a Hindu in some way? In other words, is a person who chooses to follow Christ automatically required to change his cultural address?

This is a complex and debated issue. It involves history, families, politics and labels, but Anand handles it well. He intentionally retains his cultural identity as a Hindu, but he is not bothered if someone calls him a convert to Christianity even though that is not language he chooses. For this, you have to recognize that Hinduism can be both a religious label and a cultural label. The name "Hindu" was originally derived from a word referring to the Indus River region. At one time "Hindu" was more a cultural or regional identity. Many Hindus use the native term *sanatana dharma*, meaning approximately "eternal sacred duty," to identify their religious faith.

Making a distinction between a cultural Christian (or Hindu) identity and a personal faith in Christ with our South Asian friends is essential.

Someone born in a Hindu family will likely consider Hinduism as much as a cultural identity as a religious one while outsiders tend to assume it is entirely a religious identity. But the misunderstanding goes the other way also. A Hindu is likely to see Christianity as an all-encompassing religious culture of the West including its negative associations—alcohol abuse, colonialism, divorce, sex, violence, and other vices seen on Western TV and movies. Hindus will likely form their first impressions of American Christian culture from Hollywood movies or TV and are surprised after they arrive in the U.S. to find much of it is not true. We, as true followers of Christ, are quick to distinguish the religious and cultural aspects of Christianity. *Making a distinction between a cultural Christian (or Hindu) identity and a personal faith in Christ with our South Asian friends is essential.*

This distinction is precisely the reason behind the subtitle of Anand Mahadev's story—that following Christ is not a matter of changing religious identity but a change of heart. His "conversion" to Christ was not a superficial change of culture or religion. Instead, he experienced a profound change of heart allegiance to Jesus Christ as Lord for which he is not ashamed. This is our desire and prayer: that our Hindu friends will embrace Christ as Lord from the heart for who he is and be transformed from the inside out. That is essential. A Hindu who chooses to follow Christ will learn to navigate these waters of cultural identity and family relationships with the help of the Scriptures, the Holy Spirit and other believers who have walked this road ahead of them.

▶ MISUNDERSTANDINGS

Anand further describes his cultural address as "high caste, rich and smart" and not "tribal, or poor or dim-witted." Why did he say that? Isn't that just being arrogant and boastful? No. Rather it was to cut off what he knew to be the common misunderstanding or *suspicion that those who choose to follow Christ do so for earthly gain rather than a love for Christ.* Many who have come to faith in the past few centuries have come from tribal groups or the poor. This is a reason for us to rejoice. But the perception is often that these who have "converted" have done so because becoming a "Christian" allowed them to escape a low-caste identity. Perhaps they gained access to a better education or healthcare. Or perhaps they were coerced by gifts of money or food offered by missionaries. Surely no educated, high-caste Hindu with a steady income would have any earthly reason to become a Christian, right?

An instinctive suspicion pervades the Indian social milieu... No one can be taken at face value. Everyone is suspect.

Behind these questions is a cultural element of suspicion which may reinforce this misunderstanding toward Christianity and conversion. Varma says that *"an instinctive suspicion pervades the Indian social milieu...No one can be taken at face value. Everyone is suspect."*[6] My experiences have frequently confirmed the reality of this suspicion. A Hindu student, who had chosen to follow Christ, once observed that "(Indians) are suspicious of people who are really nice." After a couple of visits to India, I too became suspicious of friendly strangers because I found they were often trying to get me to buy something or make business connections. Another Hindu friend I had known for a few years eventually shared his underlying suspicions that I was being paid by the Catholic church to convert people. I was stunned and almost laughed. But this view is widespread. Many believe that Christian workers are "in it for the money" and that it was the best job that he or she could get. Sadly, this is sometimes true in parts of South Asia.

You can imagine how these suspicions might change how the gospel message and messenger are received. We can't control what others think. But we may need to be patient with those who are suspicious of Christians. We can love and serve them unconditionally and authentically. And when such questions and suspicions arise, we can respond honestly. There is

nothing to hide. The misunderstandings Hindus have toward Christianity and those who choose to follow Christ are summarized with the acronym **"MOTIVE"** below. It should remind us that our motive must be love for Christ and for others. *But how easy it is for selfish motives and personal agendas to infect our ministry!*

 MONEY

Hindus often assume that money is the primary motive for evangelists and church leaders and for those who "convert." There are *many* vibrant churches and sacrificial ministry leaders throughout South Asia. But corruption and greed are sadly present as well. Stories abound of "rice Christians"—poor villagers who convert to Christianity to gain financially. In spite of stereotypes, the Church is growing among the poor, low caste and uneducated. Praise God for this growth! However, the students in the U.S. primarily come from a different stratum of society and retain more of this suspicion.

O ORGANIZED RELIGION

A common story line in India is that religions are primarily interested in expanding their earthly empires. The assumption is that this is the source of the money behind missionaries and church planters. This is partly understandable considering the waves of "religious empires" which have conquered parts of India over the centuries and have left their mark. Increasingly, even Hindu gurus and sects are coming under this suspicion.

T TRADITION

Religion in India is traditionally defined by birth—whether Hindu, Christian, Muslim, etc. Thus, you are defined by the religious identity and tradition of your birth family. Traditions exert a powerful influence and are rarely questioned. Changing religions can have major consequences, especially for marriage. Hindu pluralism asks why your tradition is superior to my tradition.

I IGNORANCE

Hindu culture and religion have a heritage spanning several thousand years with diverse philosophies. It can take a lifetime to learn just a portion of Hindu scriptures. Those who "convert" are assumed to be ignorant of the true teachings of Hinduism. Since most movements to Christ have been from the uneducated, this stereotype is reinforced.

V VAGUE CHRISTIAN EXAMPLES

Since religion is a cultural label of one's birth community, Hindus do not distinguish between genuine and nominal Christians much less between denominations. They may know few if any genuine believers depending on where they come from. The nearest example will define their perception.

E EGOTISM OF THE EVANGELISTS

The exclusive claims of Christ can be presented (or perceived) as cultural arrogance. Given the tradition above, "Jesus is the only way" sounds like "My culture is better than yours" or "Jesus won't accept me if I'm a Hindu." We must separate the exclusivity of Christ from cultural Christianity and share it with humility and love.

These perceptions thrive in the dark where personal contact with genuine Christ followers is lacking. Some of these will be clearer as we take a step back and look at India's complex history and religious diversity. But you don't have to understand the history and religions of the Hindu world to engage meaningfully with Hindu friends and neighbors and begin to dispel these suspicions.

▶ AUTHENTIC WITNESS

Did you notice the profound impact that a Christian friend and family had on Anand's life? Often, the starting point to dispel these suspicions is an authentic relationship with genuine followers of Jesus. Hopefully you have already had the opportunity to get to know a few South Asian friends. Fortunately, despite cultural and religious differences, it is not difficult to develop close relationships with Hindus. They are a fun group to interact with, and language barriers are rare with most high-caste, English-educated Indian international students—though not necessarily for all Hindus or South Asian immigrant communities. The growth of a transnational culture and media means we begin with more shared experiences such as movies and sports. This makes it much easier to connect over commonalities and then explore each other's cultural diversity.

Take the opportunity to get to know them both as individuals and also among their network of family and friends. Enjoy a meal together or a shared mutual interest. When possible, practice hospitality and be reciprocal—invite them into your life, but also accept invitations to enter their world. You will find that they have many positive cultural traits to teach us, such as their high value of family and relationships. And if you haven't experienced South Asian cuisines, you are in for a treat!

Spiritually, simply be authentic and open about your relationship with Christ from the beginning—not hiding that until some later point in time. This is worth emphasizing because in America we often avoid talk of politics and religion, so openness about your faith may initially feel uncomfortable. There will be more tips later in this booklet to help navigate some of the hidden aspects of culture. But *what you need above all is a willingness to reach out in love—not fearing cultural mistakes but having a willingness to ask for and accept forgiveness when you do make mistakes.* Here are a few key points to emphasize to help avoid common mistakes:

DON'T FORCE OR FAKE A FRIENDSHIP as a platform to share Christ. You can love everyone you meet, but you can't be close friends with everyone. Some people you will connect with more naturally, and friendships and relationships will grow naturally. You may not have as much in common with others but you can still love and serve them for Jesus' sake. We don't want to use friendship manipulatively. The point is to be authentic and appropriate with each person and treat them as you would want to be treated in return.

DON'T HIDE YOUR IDENTITY AS A FOLLOWER OF JESUS. You can offer to pray for them in Jesus' name or ask God's blessing on them and their family. This is usually welcomed. They need to know that you are a genuine follower of Christ and that he is an important part of your life from the beginning. If that bothers them, they will politely distance themselves from you from the outset.[7]

AFFIRM WHAT IS GOOD IN HINDU CULTURE. Be quick to see and affirm positive areas such as strong families, community values, the reality of God, and the quest for spiritual truth (Acts 17). Conversely, refrain from criticizing traditions like caste or arranged marriages.

Don't stress or overthink. Love covers a multitude of cultural mistakes. People know when they are loved even imperfectly by imperfect people. Likewise, people usually know and resent when they are being manipulated or used.

RELATIONSHIP

- *Be authentic.* Open *your life to them,* including your devotion to Christ. *Get to know their family, friends and roommates.*
- Be reciprocal in your relationships. Allow them to serve you also.
- Learn about their world. Ask them to show you their hometown using a *map of India on your phone.*
  India is a "drop in" culture, especially for close friends.
- An unplanned or last-minute visit to say "hello" or share a treat may be appreciated.

SERVICE

- Look for ways to help meet practical needs such as rides from the airport, obtaining a driver's license, or furnishing an apartment.
- Assist with rides to large department stores or Indian groceries.
- Invite them to join you in a local service project.

GATHERINGS & FUN

- Attend an Indian cultural event. Enter their world; don't just expect them to come to yours. Better yet, attend an event as a group.
- Watch a Bollywood movie together.
- Join with them to watch or play cricket and teach them about American football.

COMMUNICATION, TECHNOLOGY & SOCIAL MEDIA

- *Facebook* is a popular way of connection and communication. It also makes it easier to learn names.
- *Text messages* (by phone, *Whatsapp,* Facebook) are currently the best way to communicate.
- Except for big events, most make last minute plans. It is ok to text invitations a few days in advance or even the day of for activities.

MEN & WOMEN

Indian society is traditionally conservative. For some, this is changing, especially in cities and among the younger generation who are caught between the old and new. Indian students in the U.S. may be away from home for the first time and experiment with the new freedoms. Follow biblical standards of modesty and behavior!

Be careful in peer relationships between opposite genders:

- **Men,** don't initiate physical contact with women.
- **Women,** be modest and wise as you relate to men.

Jawaharlal Nehru, India's first prime minister, said that India is "a bundle of contradictions held together by strong but invisible threads."[8] Given India's diversity—a nation that in its modern form only came into existence in 1947—the question of national identity or what unites India is not a trivial one. There are few clear answers. It isn't language. It isn't politics. It isn't religion. Some have humorously argued that it is cricket because of the sport's popularity. But there is a shared cultural heritage which overlaps other South Asian countries of Pakistan, Bangladesh, Nepal, and Sri Lanka. Anand's story of faith illustrates the complex blend of South Asia's political, cultural, and religious heritage and the question of conversion. Did you notice the interplay between his Indian patriotism, his love for Hindu culture, yet his firm identification as a follower of Christ? A brief look at India's ancient and modern history will provide a fuller picture of this complexity and why these issues are so intertwined.

▶ ANCIENT ROOTS

The story of South Asia's history begins with the world's earliest civilizations. Admittedly, data from these early periods are limited, so dates are only approximate. The Indus Valley civilization began as early as 3500 BC situated in what is now Pakistan and Northwest India. By 2500 BC traders from these advanced cities traveled as far as Mesopotamia during the period when Abraham departed for Canaan. So Abraham's family could conceivably have walked beside Indus Valley traders. The roots of what became Hindu religions emerged from these civilizations around 1500 BC or earlier. These include the Vedas (earliest Hindu scriptures), early deities, and later the caste structure. What became Buddhism and Jainism emerged from this religious milieu around 500 BC. Over time, Buddhism became more distinct and spread beyond South Asia.

▶ KINGS AND KINGDOMS

From its earliest days, South Asia was marked by the rise and fall of dynasties and empires, small and great, originating both from inside and outside the Indian subcontinent. Political control tended to revert to localized kings except during periods of more powerful, expansionist dynasties. *Each of these empires left their own cultural, political, and religious imprints on future generations.*

From the outside, the Persian empire, followed by the Greek empire under Alexander the Great, conquered parts of modern day Pakistan and the Indus Valley. From the inside, local dynasties grew in power and took control of large regions. The most notable is the Mauryan empire (300s BC), which re-captured the lands that Alexander the Great had ruled. In fact, only the much later Mughul and British empires ruled larger areas. The Mauryan empire reached its height under the emperor Ashoka in a period marked by flourishing art but also bloodshed in his territorial expansion. Reportedly, after seeing so much warfare, the emperor renounced violence and converted to Buddhism, making it the state religion. He sent Buddhist missionaries beyond the borders of India, perhaps as far as Egypt and Greece, and his own family members carried Buddhism to Sri Lanka.[9] While Buddhism is only a tiny minority in India today, the official seal of India today is the four-headed lion pillar from Ashoka's empire.

The later Gupta empire in the North (4th to 6th centuries AD) represented a golden age for Hindu civilization. It was marked by developments in art, literature and mathematics, notably the concepts of zero and infinity. The South retained its own distinctive culture due to its isolation from the invasions which North India repeatedly encountered. But it had ongoing contact with other civilizations with lucrative trade as far as Rome and Egypt. The Hindu Chola dynasty in the south lasted for about 1,000 years, and its navy-controlled territory as far as Malaysia and Indonesia. Consequently, it spread elements of Tamil culture, literature, and religion throughout its kingdom.

सत्यमेव जयते

India's national seal which features the 3rd century BC pillar from Ashoka's empire.

Sometime in this early period, churches were established along the southwest (Malabar) coast which included high caste Hindu families. Church tradition connects these to the apostle Thomas. Precise history is difficult, and how much these communities grew beyond this region is uncertain. Though they had indigenous roots, these churches became linked and governed by the Eastern Persian church (Syriac) by the 5th century. A 6th century visitor observed that the Indian church *"was only a tiny minority community, a separated, distinctive cultural island in a vast non-Christian sea."*[10] Nevertheless, this ancient Indian Christian community did endure in the southern tip of the subcontinent and was present when European traders arrived over a millennium later.[11]

▶ ISLAM

Islamic kingdoms began to impact the region around AD 1000 and kings from Afghanistan captured Delhi in the 12th century. Muslim and Hindu kingdoms clashed in the next two centuries, though more in a quest for power rather than religious reasons. However, some contested sacred religious sites from this period became flashpoints for religious and communal violence. The Mughal period beginning in the 16th century brought an end to much of the warfare and fostered religious tolerance. Though Islamic from Central Asia, the Mughals integrated Hindus into their administration. Akbar, one of its most powerful emperors, used interfaith marriage alliances with the remaining independent Hindu kingdoms to strengthen his empire and engaged in religious discussions with those of other faiths, including Catholic priests. The Taj Mahal represents the crowning beauty of Mughal architecture from this period.

▶ EUROPEAN COLONIALISM

During the Mughal empire, the Portuguese reached India and captured trading ports in Goa by 1511, one hundred years before any other European power. They initially dominated trade, and Jesuit missionaries introduced Catholicism. They eventually established schools and hospitals, which are a respected legacy to this day. Most who joined these Catholic churches came from tribal and low-caste backgrounds, which created islands of Catholic subcultures but with little impact on majority Hindu and Muslim populations. By the 1600s, the British East India Company arrived and dominated trade. Power later shifted from the "company" to the British "crown." By the 19th century, Indian states were ruled by local authorities, but the British maintained centralized control mainly for the sake of financial profit. The early Protestant missionary work began in this period. Churches, hospitals, schools, and elements of social reform were established primarily among the lower castes. But too often the work retained European cultural forms of worship and dress. *There remains a strong association between Western colonialism and Christianity even today. Furthermore, Christianity is often equated with an outward cultural expression rather than a living, personal faith, and missionaries are often assumed to be expanding their religious empires.*

There remains a strong association between Western colonialism and Christianity even today.

▶ INDEPENDENCE

The British empire left its mark on South Asia with a sprawling bureaucracy, an extensive railway system, and widespread use of English. But its emphasis on profit and management left some populations impoverished and fueled resentment of foreign rule. Resentment led to revolt from the mid-1800s and ultimately independence in 1947. Mohandas (called Mahatma) Gandhi led political opposition through peaceful resistance against the British. But as the independence movement grew so did religious fractures. Radical Hindu parties were opposed to Gandhi's religious tolerance and power sharing with Muslims. Similarly, some Muslim groups feared being a minority in a Hindu controlled state.

Tensions between radical Hindus and Muslims continued even as Gandhi and the British pushed for a united, secular India. Tensions won out and two states were created effective on August 15, 1947—the Hindu majority India and the Muslim majority Pakistan. At the time, Pakistan was a united country but geographically split into East and West Pakistan. East Pakistan later became independent Bangladesh after a war in 1971.

The new political borders created major disruptions and mass migrations. Many Muslims fled to Pakistan while Hindus in Pakistan fled to India. Worse than mere displacement was communal violence and bloodshed. The wealthy and agriculturally rich region of Punjab was split down the middle and religious communities fled both ways across the border. Entire trainloads of Hindus and Sikhs crossing the border to India were stopped and slaughtered by Muslims. Similarly, trainloads of Muslims traveling to Pakistan were slaughtered by Hindu and Sikh mobs. *By the time the dust settled 10 million people had changed sides of the border and half a million were killed in the violence.*[12]

War broke out between India and Pakistan over the disputed Kashmir region just a few months after independence. It remains disputed and armed skirmishes continue to happen there from time to time. Stakes became even higher after both nations obtained nuclear weapons in the 1990s. There are efforts to promote peace between the countries, but tensions remain.

Mahatma Gandhi

In the most recent decades, India's economic development and cultural change has come at a dizzying pace. For the most part, *secularism and religious tolerance are the general rule among middle class and educated Hindus.* However, tensions simmer between Hindu and Muslim radicals. Violence still breaks out and competing ideologies fight over political control. Political power shifts back and forth between a more secular, religiously tolerant vision and radical Hindu groups who want India to be religiously Hindu. It is notable that Gandhi, a Hindu, was assassinated by a radical Hindu just a year after independence. So the "bundle of contradictions" of South Asia's complicated religious and political history still marks modern India.

There also remains an undercurrent of opposition and suspicion toward Christian ministry, especially in many local regions. The recently elected

Hindu fundamentalist political party restricts foreign missionary work and foreign aid money from Christian organizations. A few states have anti-conversion laws, which are aimed at preventing religious coercion but can be loosely interpreted. Among educated Hindu students there seems to be a growing skepticism and fatigue with religions in general. Secularism, atheism, or pluralism are more appealing alternatives.

KEY POINTS

- Religion, culture, and politics are often intertwined in South Asian history and not always distinguished.

- Religion has sometimes been a source or excuse for violence and division. Pluralism and secularism are popular alternatives.

- Christianity retains colonial and Western associations (British or Catholic) even though Christianity reached the southern tip of South Asia long before the colonial period.

- Evangelism can be confused with colonialism, politics, or financial gain. These entanglements need to be removed when sharing the gospel.

- Terms like **Christianity**, **missionary**, and **conversion** carry unintended cultural and historical baggage and *should be avoided or carefully defined to minimize misunderstandings.*

It should be clear now that South Asia is really a collection of peoples and states—more akin to a European Union—except more complex. There are estimates of more than 3,000 distinct people groups with over 2,200 classified as unreached.[13] If you take caste and religious divisions into account, the complexity is truly dizzying. This diversity helps explain why people like Anand often introduce themselves with their "cultural address." This chapter provides a simple grid to grasp the big pieces of this diversity. There is a horizontal (geographic) diversity from one region to another and vertical (social or caste) diversity you find from person to person within the same location. Note that, if you are encountering South Asians primarily in North America, the caste diversity issues are minimal. As you meet people, you can ask them more about what is unique and important to them.

▶ HORIZONTAL DIVERSITY

The most notable ethnic division is between North and South India; more than 95% of the population falls within these two ethnic groupings. Other significant divisions are those primarily near Nepal and northeastern states which have more Tibetan and Chinese heritage. The following descriptions may be a helpful place to start to understand India's regional diversity.[14]

SOUTH INDIA The peoples of South India have a common Dravidian linguistic and cultural heritage. These are in the five states of Kerala, Tamil Nadu, Andhra Pradesh, Telangana, and Karnataka. The major languages spoken are Malayalam, Tamil, Telugu (for both Andhra Pradesh and Telangana), and Kannada, respectively. English is quite common and may be preferred to Hindi. These areas generally have more Christian influence. The people of Sri Lanka have some cultural similarities but are a majority Buddhist country. Major cities in this region are Chennai, Bangalore, and Hyderabad—the last two being the "Silicon Valleys" of India with thriving multi-national companies.

NORTH INDIA The peoples of North India predominantly share an Indo-Aryan linguistic and cultural heritage. The region includes 75% of the country's population and the most densely populated states. Hindi is the most common language spoken in the North along with many related languages and dialects. While the central part of North India is considered the Hindu heartland, there are significant Muslim populations as well.

MAP OF INDIA

PAKISTAN

JAMMU & KASHMIR

CHINA

PAKISTAN

HIMACHAL PRADESH

PUNJAB

UTTARAKHAND

HARYANA
Delhi

CHINA

NEPAL

ARUNACHAL PRADESH

RAJASTHAN

UTTAR PRADESH

SIKKIM

BHUTAN

ASSAM

NAGALAND

BIHAR

MEGHALAYA

MANIPUR

Ahmedabad

MADHYA PRADESH

JHARK-HAND

WEST BENGAL

BANGLADESH

TRIPURA

MIZORAM

GUJARAT

Kolkata (Calcutta)

MYANMAR

Surat

DADRA & NAGAR HAVELI

MAHARASHTRA

CHHATTISGARH

ODISHA

Mumbai (Bombay)

Pune

TELANGANA

Hyderabad

Vishakhapatum

GOA

KARNATAKA

ANDHRA PRADESH

Bay of Bengal

Bengaluru (Bangalore)

Chennai (Madras)

Arabian Sea

TAMIL NADU

PUDUCHERRY

ANDAMAN & NICOBAR ISLANDS

KERALA

SRI LANKA

INDIAN OCEAN

REGIONS*

- ● South India
- ● Northeast India
- ● ● ● North India
- ● Western India
- ● Eastern India

*No official or universally accepted definitions of India's regions exist.

© 2019 InterVarsity Christian Fellowship/USA

Delhi is the largest city in the region. New Delhi is India's national capital and one of eleven districts within the city of Delhi. The peoples of Nepal are related to those of the North but with their own distinctive ethnic and cultural blends.

WESTERN INDIA While generally associated with North India, it is helpful to distinguish the Western states including Maharashtra and Gujarat. Maharashtra is home to Mumbai (formerly Bombay), the largest city of India and its financial center. It has a thriving, global movie industry nicknamed "Bollywood." The neighboring state of Gujarat is also an influential financial and business area, and many among the Indian diaspora come from this state.

EASTERN INDIA Generally associated with North India, this region neighbors Bangladesh and shares a common Bengali language and culture. Bengal is known for contributions to the arts and literature from intellectuals such as Vivekananda and Rabindranath Tagore. Calcutta is the largest city in this area—the original place of Mother Theresa's ministry.

NORTHEAST INDIA The region of Northeast India is geographically isolated from the rest of the political borders of India. Many people groups in this region are ethnically related to Chinese and Tibetan peoples along with indigenous tribal groups. There are significant numbers of Christians in this region, though predominantly from tribal backgrounds.

▶ DIASPORA DIVERSITY

It is important to note that there is generally a wide gap between Indian international students and the children of Indian families that were born or predominantly raised in the U.S. Like other cultural groups (Korean American, Japanese American, etc.), second generation Indians will likely have a dual identity which varies from person to person. They are American with an Indian identity that is incorporated to varying degrees depending on their family's cultural isolation, length of time in the U.S., personal preferences, and other factors. Varma noted that immigrants from South Asian countries tend to integrate less than those from other countries and may even retain religious rituals that have been forgotten in India.[15] Sam George's book, *Coconut Generation*, highlights the distinctive characteristics of this group. Overall, South Asian students do not *automatically* identify with second-generation Indians. But with a dual cultural identity, willing second-generation Indians *can* serve as bridge builders with the South Asian community.

▶ VERTICAL DIVERSITY

Anand Mahadev identified the vertical dimension of his cultural address in the first line of his story in chapter 1. He is from a Brahmin family—the highest caste within Hinduism—and socially not tribal or poor. This was to dispel the suspicion that earthly motives drove him to embrace Christ. It also illustrates the vertical dimension of South Asia's complex world. Caste compounds the diversity of South Asia because it stratifies society vertically within each grouping and not simply horizontally through language and geography. Outside of the South Asian context, caste is widely known, little understood, and often condemned. Christians in America may have heard of the plight of the Dalits, or untouchable caste, and their movements to Christianity. We should rejoice and praise God for any genuine movements to Christ whether large or small. However, fewer would be aware of previous anti-caste movements. In fact, Dr. Ambedkar, who authored India's constitution in 1947, was an Oxford educated member of one of the untouchable castes. He eventually converted to Buddhism to escape the confines of caste.

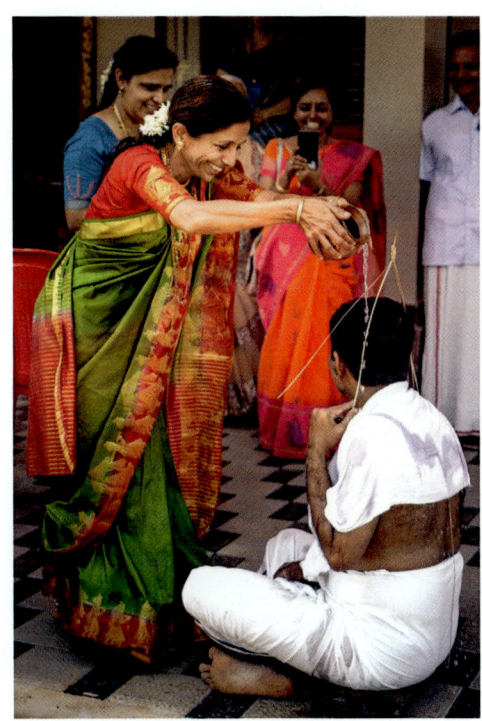

One danger is that earthly motives can be associated with these movements and create confusion for those from higher castes and the middle class who have more to lose socially for following Christ. Thus, Anand was also quick to add that he was not coerced, deceived or financially induced to follow Christ.

Traditionally, there were four broad caste groupings. The top three castes represent about 15% (5% each) of India's population and are commonly considered "high-caste Hindus." The fourth category (*shudras*) is largely ignored and is classified officially as the OBC (Other Backward Castes). The remaining groups are listed by the government as Scheduled Castes and Scheduled Tribes (aboriginal

Ritual for a Brahmin man wearing his sacred thread

peoples). The Scheduled Castes were named as "untouchables" and are self-titled "*Dalits*" (literally "the oppressed ones"). However, these broad divisions are more theory than reality or practice. Instead, within these groupings are *thousands of sub-castes, or* jati, *which vie for prominence and are more significant for communal identity and practice.*[16]

Generally, it is better not to initiate questions of caste with South Asian students...

Caste is a sensitive and changing issue with a long, complex history, and it is not easily reduced to a simple right or wrong formula. It cannot be simply equated to wealth or education or discrimination in every case. Although it may have ancient roots in Hindu culture, it is present across society and religions including Christianity. Even anti-caste religious movements like Jainism and Sikhism still have castes. In modern India, the influence of caste is changing and diminishing. Nevertheless, it still delineates families and stratifies communities most often in delimiting who a person can and cannot marry. In the worst cases, inter-caste violence sometimes erupts in villages along with competition for political power. So it is better to include it here as an aspect of the cultural rather than religious diversity.

Generally, *it is better not to initiate questions of caste with South Asian students unless they bring it up or among those you know well.* It might feel like someone from another country asking you about racial problems in America and affirmative action. If you are from America that would probably make you uncomfortable because it is in part a historically painful issue that has impacted successive generations. Now it is a complex and sometimes painful social and political issue, and solutions are not always simple. In fact, a caste-based reservation system (a more complex form of affirmative action) is used at educational institutions in India.

▶ THE ROLE OF CASTE TODAY

On one hand, modernization and education are breaking down many social stigmas and caste divisions. Students rightly point out positive developments and the diminishing negative role of caste especially in urban areas. But social stratification remains a part of everyday life, and the prospect is bleak for those in the lowest castes who are locked into poverty. While Hindu students identify as middle class, *they overwhelmingly come from urban, high-caste families.* They are more "elite" than a middle-class identity would indicate and represent only a narrow slice of the whole.[17]

Practically, then, *caste distinctions are minor among Hindu international students* because most come from similar social strata. Very few from the lower castes have had the same opportunities. But *this mobile and global student population has great potential for positive influence* on the future of the South Asian world.

For students, *caste will likely relate most to marriage.* The role caste plays in matrimonial choices varies greatly among families. Some are more progressive and do not consider caste. But for many, caste is an important factor in potential marriage partners. For Hindu students who come to faith, this issue of who they can marry becomes amplified. In fact, a family who hears that their son or daughter has "become a Christian" may initially assume they "converted" to marry a Christian. *Again, the confusion of earthly and spiritual motives for following Christ arises.*

Ultimately, it is not our responsibility to change the social structure of South Asia. Our privilege is to share the gospel without discrimination and allow the gospel to transform society, beginning with the hearts of individual men and women.

KEY POINTS

- A family's regional origin is very influential in their cultural identity and impacts their knowledge of genuine Christian faith. Some regions and people groups have little to no relevant witness while others have historic churches present or nearby.

- When it comes to issues of caste and South Asian Hindu students in the U.S., you can generally *assume that they are from high-caste families.*

- Changes are taking place related to caste, but it remains a restrictive reality for many from the lower castes in South Asia.

- *You should generally NOT initiate discussions of caste.* This is a complex and sensitive topic and would feel like someone asking about racism in the U.S.

- Ethnic and caste diversity is most influential in marriage and family relationships.

- For a more thorough introduction to this topic see *Disciple Making Among Hindus: Making Authentic Relationships Grow* by Tim Shultz and *Hinduism* by H. L. Richard.

4 HINDU CULTURE AND WORLDVIEWS

Authentic, cross-cultural relationships involve the joy of learning about another person's culture and world. It is exciting to share and experience diverse aspects of culture such as food, clothing, music, and dance. Initially, the differences may seem obvious, like the spice level of foods. Over time, however, you realize that there are deeper differences that affect communication, assumptions, and values. Patty Lane likens culture and worldview to an iceberg in which there are obvious differences visible above the water (objective culture) but also deeper differences hidden below (subjective culture).[18]

Communication styles are one example that lies just below the surface which you will encounter as you relate to those from the Hindu world. Direct communication is common in North America in which you "say what you mean" and "mean what you say." In much of Asia, including South Asia, indirect communication is more normal in which a person may answer indirectly or "around" a difficult issue to avoid giving a painful or direct answer. Those native to these cultures usually pick up the intended meaning quite naturally, but outsiders can easily miss it.

While it would have been obvious to a cultural insider, it was not clear to us.

To give a humorous example, on one visit to India our small team of Americans visited a university campus and then wanted to get a bite to eat in the canteen. We weren't sure if it would be clean enough for our American stomachs, so we asked our hosts. They said that it might be ok but suggested several other options. Noting that the menu items looked tasty, we inquired again and received a similar response. Honestly, we weren't sure if they were in hurry to leave or if a snack would be ok, and several of us were quite hungry. So we decided it would be faster to get a bite to eat there. The next morning half of the team was out of commission with stomach issues. When we met our hosts the next day, we curiously asked one of our hosts, "Why didn't you tell us the food there wouldn't be good?" Without hesitating, he replied, "We told you three times not to eat there!" While it would have been obvious to a cultural insider, it was not clear to us. He didn't want to directly say that the food might not be good for us, so he told us indirectly and expected us to pick up on what he meant. We were all fine within twenty-four hours, and we learned a valuable lesson about cultural differences and assumptions.

This is not the place to explain all the cultural differences that exist in South Asia. Many cultural elements you simply learn as you go. But a few noteworthy objective elements of South Asian culture are helpful to know initially and are summarized in the chart to the right. For a fuller exploration of cross-cultural issues, see *A Beginner's Guide to Crossing Cultures* by Patty Lane or *Figuring Foreigners Out* by Craig Storti.

These are some outward layers of culture and worldview. They are important as we relate cross-culturally to minimize miscommunication and confusion. But worldview and identity go much deeper than food and communication styles. Worldview involves assumptions about reality and how people think.[20] These deeper elements of worldview may relate to how the gospel is most naturally understood. A look at some of the worldview and identity issues for the Hindu world may help distinguish between cultural and spiritual issues, between important and minor issues, and may suggest helpful approaches for authentic witness and discipleship.

Katie Rawson has summarized three worldviews which influence students today: traditional or pre-modern, modern, and post-modern. Traditional worldviews emphasize the *value of tradition and the elders*. Modern worldviews emphasize the *value of science for determining truth*. Post-modernism rejects elements of both and *values individual experience to determine truth*. Notably, both traditional and post-modern worldviews give priority to relationships though in different ways.[21]

South Asian students today display values from of each of these worldviews. They may follow a traditional worldview pattern with their family and community, thus

CULTURAL TIPS[19]

FOOD IS IMPORTANT

Food is a delicious part of South Asian culture with great regional variety. Sharing a meal together is a great way to begin to connect. Accept an offer of *chai* (tea) and ask someone to teach you how to make it. Cook an Indian meal together or visit an Indian restaurant.

Hindus have a variety of practices regarding diet. There is no need to be anxious—just ask. If you are hosting it is best to:
- Avoid serving beef or pork (chicken is a good option).
- Provide some vegetarian food.

HOSPITALITY

- Hospitality is valued in South Asia. If you visit them, they may bring you a drink or snack without asking. This is basic hospitality.
- If they are visiting you, they may initially decline offers of food or a drink. Offer more than once.

GROUP ORIENTATION

While individualistic values are rising, South Asians tend to be group-oriented.
- Decisions are often made as a group.
- When possible, include them in the process of making decisions. It may take longer, but it will give ownership.
- Plans may change at the last minute because they prioritize relationships over scheduled appointments.

INDIRECT COMMUNICATION

- South Asians find it difficult and disrespectful to say "no" directly. They may say yes in front of you and then not show up or call at the last minute to decline.
- More often they will say "maybe." Maybe usually means "no."
- Be respectful and gentle if you need to decline and say "no" to them.

TIME ORIENTATION

- Indian society is less time oriented and more relationship oriented. Plans often remain fluid until the last minute. Be prepared to adjust and don't be easily offended. (see learningindia.in/time-is-eternal/)

SOCIAL OBLIGATION

- "Thank you" is rarely expressed verbally. It sounds artificial. Gratitude is traditionally expressed by reciprocal actions.

being willing to accept an arranged marriage or follow their parents' direction for vocational choices. At the same time, their scientific (modern) education has caused them to question traditional religious beliefs. And they may adopt more global and post-modern, individualistic values which allow them to flourish in global work environments. This interwoven web of worldview assumptions creates a complex identity in today's generation of Hindu students.

▶ HINDU IDENTITY

How would a South Asian or Hindu student (consciously or unconsciously) answer the question "Who am I?" given the complexity of the Indian world? The diagram here suggests a simplified way to consider Hindu identity and the various worldview influences on it. Every nation and people group is unique—how much more so, an individual person? This

is only a generalized model, and these layers are interconnected.[22] Nevertheless, the diversity of Indian culture and identity presents a special challenge, especially to cultural outsiders. Indian author Varma noted that "the Indian persona is a layered accretion; like an onion, the outer layer is never the only one."[23]

The layers of this diagram move from the more surface-level identity to the most substantial and influential. First is the **GLOBAL (TRANSNATIONAL) IDENTITY** that has grown significantly in recent years. Most Hindu students today come from urban, high-caste families, often having worked in multinational companies where western culture and values are common. This group of engineering and information technology (IT) professionals numbers only about two million out of India's labor force of 480 million but exerts great influence economically and socially. Radhakrishnan suggests that they are collectively redefining what it means to be Indian.[24] While this is the outermost identity layer, it should not be minimized because *it is simultaneously influencing and redefining the core elements of Indian identity.*

Next is the **NATIONAL IDENTITY** which has both new and old elements. India as a nation is only half a century old, but the association of the Indian people with the land goes back for millennia. It is not a trivial matter to

define what characteristics make a person an Indian. This layer involves appropriate patriotism but is complicated by current politics. Those from other South Asian countries like Nepal will experience different national influences unique to their political history.

Deeper still is the **RELIGIOUS IDENTITY**. Here it is specifically Hindu but could be any religious identity such as Christian, Hindu or Muslim. There are varying and often debated degrees to which an individual religious community is considered "Indian" or not. The Hindutva (Hindu nationalist) movement equates being Indian with being Hindu. So the distinction for a Hindu between these two layers is noted by a dotted line. This religious identity refers to a person's religious "community" *without reference to personal beliefs. Recognizing this distinction is critical,* and it is part of the fine line that Anand Mahadev walked in his patriotism and appreciation for Hindu culture versus Hindu religious nationalism.

Near the core is the **FAMILY IDENTITY**, where a person historically finds their deepest sense of identity. It is not chosen but is defined by birth. This identity includes the language, ethnicity, caste, and relational responsibilities which stem from a person's birth community. Traditionally it defined the broader community of people with whom one could marry, and it is the community who would be most deeply shamed by a person's "conversion." Anand's family identity would be Tamil Brahmin narrowing down to his immediate and extended family. In the past this has been similar to biblical culture in which birth order determines family responsibilities and inheritance rights as well as whom to marry and who decides whom one can marry. But with the rise of globalization and transnational influences, the strength of family influence is changing and there is a growing generation gap. Further, the influence of peer friends is frequently higher, whether or not they are a part of the family and ethnic community. This changing relationship between individual and family is shown with a dotted line on the diagram.

Finally, at the center is a person's **INDIVIDUAL IDENTITY** which includes their spiritual beliefs. Naturally, it is the most important and is as varied as the number of individuals in India. Again, note that a *person's spiritual beliefs may differ dramatically from their religious label.* People may keep this private from all but those closest to them or it may be unquestioned. Remember that in Anand Mahadev's story, while he was born in a Hindu family (religious identity), he never connected with the traditional practices of his family. When his friend introduced him to Christ, he embraced him as Lord—not as a new religious identity label but as a life transformed at the heart level. By his own admission he had no religion. Following this heart-level transformation, he knew his identity was now in Christ but was less concerned about the superficial religious label.

- Religious debates and comparisons rarely go very far. It is okay to discuss the differences between Hinduism and Christianity. But when you ask "What do Hindus believe?" you are more likely to get standard answers that they have heard others say about Hinduism. This is simply information exchange. But don't assume that they embrace all that they are saying. They may simply be explaining their cultural heritage or trying to be helpful to you.

- You can engage people in spiritual discussions at all levels, *but your ultimate focus should be at the heart level.*

- To reach heart issues, ask open-ended questions about their belief in God, purpose in life, method of prayer, etc. The goal is not to compare a set of beliefs and persuade them to exchange one set of beliefs and traditions for another. Rather, it is to help them reflect on the heart level questions of life and introduce the person and work of Christ.

▶ EMERGING GENERATION

The impact of globalism on Hindu identity for the younger generation is worth a closer look. More and more students are outwardly Westernized and individualistic compared to the generation of students before them. They have grown up shaped by global media and are no longer culturally isolated. They may have grown up playing cricket but might now prefer basketball or soccer. They may have grown up going to the temple with their parents, but now they read atheists like Richard Dawkins or websites like thelogicalindian.com. I was welcoming several new 20-something-aged students to our city and asked them what movies they liked best. To my surprise they all said they preferred Hollywood to Bollywood (Indian) movies. Similarly, a colleague in New York City was eager to show contextual hospitality to some new students and invited them for *chai* (Indian tea). One student replied, "If I wanted *chai*, I would have stayed in India. Let's go get a beer!"

There are positive opportunities with this change but also dangers that we need to recognize. Positively, the cultural overlap in the new global culture makes relational connection more natural and faster. There is now a greater pool of shared knowledge, media, and experiences. It is simply easier to connect based on that shared experience. Students are often more open to friendships with non-Indians and curious about the world—both American culture and other cultures. More Hindu students are open to attending multiethnic or American Christian meetings out of spiritual or cultural curiosity or to spend time with new friends. Some are more tolerant of our cross-cultural mistakes or less fearful of discussing deeper spiritual questions. Thus, it is possible that this generation may be more open to individualistic evangelistic methods than previous generations.

Praise God for the opportunities and openness. But *we don't want to underestimate the differences in identity and worldview that lie below the surface.* Most importantly, we want to make sure that gospel communication and transformation takes place at the heart level and not the superficial global level. If a student perceives and embraces Christian faith as part of American global culture, then their faith may only

be superficial as well. What may appear to be a sincere embrace of the gospel may be only a cultural embrace or a temporary openness to new spiritual things. It may be an honest step but only a first step. Katie Rawson's research among East Asians showed a disturbing pattern in which surface level conversion led to short-lived discipleship. When students returned to their home culture or God stopped answering their prayers, they quit following

Jesus.[25] God can certainly change someone's heart in a brief encounter, but it is much easier for cross-cultural misunderstandings to occur when there is no context or when the deeper heart issues are unknown or ignored.

A related danger is that if our discipleship is predominantly individualistic we can unintentionally sever the connections which would allow the gospel to flow naturally to their family. So even if a new Hindu background believer clearly distinguishes between Western culture and genuine faith in Christ, they may underestimate that identification in their parents' minds. Or they may have understood and embraced the gospel in a form that resonates with the secular, global context, but they may not know how to share that cross-generationally with their family. So it is important for them to wrestle with what it looks like to live out and communicate their faith to their own Indian community and family.

There are twin dangers. If gospel transformation doesn't take root at the heart level, the pull of the secular, global world may sever any meaningful ability for a new Hindu believer to share with their family. Or else the gravitational pull of family and tradition may attract a person back into the more familiar Hindu world, and they will cease to follow Christ. As Varma wrote, "The hold of tradition on Indians should never be underestimated. Tradition and technology sleep in the same bed in India."[26] Ultimately, the gospel must transform every level from the heart outward (Rom. 12:1-3).

- Positively, the shared global culture makes relational connections easier and individualized gospel methods more accessible.

- Negatively, if gospel communication and transformation doesn't reach the heart level, it may not last or it may isolate new believers from their family and sever natural avenues for gospel communication.

▶ VALUE SYSTEMS

How do we plant the gospel deeply and avoid surface level changes? A partial answer is that it doesn't ultimately depend on us but on the power of the gospel itself (Rom. 1:16), the work of the Holy Spirit (John 16:8), and the hearer's response (Mark 4:1-20). Elsewhere, Jesus speaks of the farmer who does not know how the seed works to grow but still he participates in

the harvest. This should give us freedom as we lovingly share knowing that we are simply farmers. The power is in the seed.

At the same time, the examples of Jesus and Paul and others throughout the New Testament show a passion to communicate the gospel well, even contextually, to the needs of the audience. Jesus engaged people differently according to their needs and knowledge. Notice how differently Jesus shared with Nicodemus (John 3) who knew the Jewish law and the Samaritan woman with limited background in the very next chapter. Paul, though a Jew, went to great lengths to understand his Gentile hearers (Acts 17) and to live out and communicate the gospel in a way that would be most helpful for the salvation of his hearers.

The diversity of worldviews suggests that there are likely a variety of differences below the surface. The objective and subjective aspects of culture and worldview were noted above. But others are deeper and relate to what the culture values and impact how the gospel is most naturally understood.

Roland Muller has proposed a three-fold set of cultural values which are *emotional* effects of sin seen since the fall of Adam and Eve. These are guilt/innocence, honor/shame, and fear/power. When Adam and Eve sinned, they felt guilty, they felt ashamed of their nakedness, and they hid in fear from God and each other (Gen. 3). Muller's study suggests that cultures typically have one of these as a dominant value system but are often a blend. These value systems are summarized below.[27]

GUILT/INNOCENCE "How do I get rid of a guilty conscience?" or "What is right/wrong?" This view has dominated 20th century U.S. culture in which the rule of law is held highly and a sense of guilt or innocence is internalized. So when you are stopped by a policeman, someone from a guilt-based culture will likely feel guilty or wonder what law they have broken. Many Western evangelistic methods begin with the assumption that others have a guilty conscience for breaking God's law and a need for forgiveness and cleansing. This is true. But not all cultures start from this assumption. In fact, some Hindus who have embraced Christ as Savior and Lord noted that they didn't fully understand their sin and guilt until after they became believers.

HONOR/SHAME "How to I maintain the honor of my community?" or "How do I avoid bringing shame to my family?" This is more complicated for westerners to grasp, and Muller uses lying as an example. In honor/shame cultures a lie is not necessarily a right or wrong issue. Rather, is what is said honorable? If a lie protects a group's honor, it is good; but if it is said for selfish reasons, it is wrong. Similarly, in honor/shame cultures it is not uncommon to hear that "stealing is wrong only if you get caught." That means that a person may steal and not feel guilty about it because it is wrong. But if they get caught, it brings shame on the family, which is deeply painful. This view is common in the Middle East, Far East, and parts of South Asia.

FEAR/POWER "How do I obtain spiritual power to get what I need in life? or "How do I avoid the influence of evil powers?" This is traditionally most prominent in tribal cultures with shamans or those who can interact with and influence the spiritual realm. The roots of Hinduism are animistic and many traditional Hindu practices involve rituals and amulets in the pursuit of blessing from the gods. It is probably strongest in the villages but influences all levels of society. Varma noted that even educated engineers and scientists still follow astrology and wear amulets to ward off evil spirits. Among the younger generation these practices are gradually being discarded. But the influence of fear/power remains even if it is below the surface.

▶ HOW VALUE SYSTEMS AFFECT HINDU STUDENTS

The diversity of South Asia suggests a blend of value systems depending on regional differences and backgrounds. Those from a Christian background may be more familiar with guilt-based values. Those from Muslim families may reflect a dominant honor/shame worldview. Among the Hindu majority the worldview is probably a blend of fear/power with respect to God and honor/shame with respect to their family and immediate community. Yet the emerging generation of Hindu students may include more guilt-based values and pursuit of truth based on the scientific education and Western influences.

So, if the layers of South Asian identity above are accurate, we might expect these values to influence an individual in *differing degrees, relationships, and orders*. Global South Asians are accustomed to Western and individualistic modes of thought and may increasingly respond to guilt-based gospel presentations. They may be motivated by a pursuit of truth or knowledge. But since law and sin is typically not so prominent or seen in relation to God, it may not always communicate fully.

At the religious level, some Hindu practices reflect fear/power values even for those who aren't religious. So even those who are atheist or agnostic may respond to difficulties with a need for spiritual power. A bright engineering student from Nepal staunchly identified as an atheist Hindu. But upon graduation he encountered a difficult job search and faced the possibility of returning home deeply in debt. At the last minute, he received a job offer and was relieved. On his first visit home, he gave a large offering at a temple in gratitude for the answered prayer.

Many Hindus who have become followers of Jesus have experienced the power and goodness of God in answered prayer or miraculous deliverance. One student's life was spared after a serious car accident in India. He knew that he should not have survived and that believers and the power of Jesus were instrumental in his recovery. Years later, after significant wrestling, he surrendered his life to Christ. That deliverance marked a turning point in his journey to faith. Notice that his first experience of God's kindness was not relief from a guilty conscience but the need for power and rescue in weakness (Rom. 2:4). In fact, Hindus may view sin as weakness, ignorance, or impurity which keeps them from receiving God's blessings and power. Still, everyone must ultimately realize that our deepest need is deliverance from the power of sin and death.

If gospel communication and transformation doesn't reach the heart level, it may not last

If the core of South Asian identity is family, then we might expect honor/shame to be significant as well. Family remains the enduring core of Hindu identity even as society and culture change. Honor/shame values aren't as pervasive as in the Middle East or East Asia. In some Middle Eastern families, honor killings are condoned to preserve family honor. In East Asia, saving face permeates society. In South Asia, Hindu families seek to uphold the reputation of their immediate family in the community but don't go as far to "save face" in situations beyond the family community.

Honor/shame values suggest additional ways to communicate the gospel and the challenges facing disciples from Hindu families. For one, sin may be shared as a failure to honor God relationally and not abstractly as a lawgiver. Parables such as the Prodigal Son provide a relational depiction of sin as the son shamefully rejects his own father and wants only his money. We had a group of Hindu students act out the story of the Prodigal Son while a narrator read the story from the Bible. Most had never heard the story before. When the narrator read about the son asking for his inheritance there was an audible gasp in the room. They were shocked by the son shaming his father.

Secondly, those who dishonor their family, perhaps by marrying an unacceptable partner or changing religion, face the shame of social and emotional ostracism. When a Hindu chooses to follow Jesus, it will likely bring shame to the family in the eyes of the community. This is a painful experience for everyone involved. Did you notice in Anand Mahadev's story above the pains he took to show how much he valued his Hindu culture and loved his grandfather? This is not hyperbole but genuine affection. It was likely painful for him as he felt like he was hurting or dishonoring his family. And it is likely that the family would be ashamed in their community if their son turned his back on their faith—especially since he was from a priestly family whose role was to uphold the religious rituals for the community.

While it may take time, it is critical that a new believer from a Hindu family learns to embrace and reconcile their new faith with their cultural identity as a Hindu. They will want to leave behind the religious rituals and gods of their past, but that doesn't mean they must abandon their family and the aspects of Hindu culture that are not religious. Each individual will wrestle with how and when to share with their family. This may take time, but fellowship with other Hindu background believers can help them navigate these waters and discover what it means to honor Christ while loving their family as well.

KEY POINTS

- Recognize that Hindu students are impacted by diverse worldview values and they may *compartmentalize* their beliefs.

- Present the gospel using a variety of biblical stories and analogies which communicate sin and the gospel in each worldview.

- Share your testimony. But don't assume that the concepts that are most significant in your journey will be the same for them. Share other aspects of your faith story—perhaps a time when God showed his power and love when you felt weak and fearful.

- Don't expect a uniform order in those who come to faith. Some will initially pursue questions of truth while others may experience God's loving power first instead.

- Help new believers understand the depth of the gospel at each of these levels and especially as it relates to family and identity.

When we meet Hindus, we are quick to ask or wonder, "What do you believe?" But this first assumes a systematic set of beliefs exists. It doesn't. It also assumes that a consistent religious belief system is a priority for them. It isn't.

▶ HINDUISM OVERVIEW

Hinduism in its modern form may be better defined by what it is not rather than what it is. It is not creedal. It has no founder. It has no single common scripture. It does not claim an absolute truth—except perhaps that there is no absolute truth. It values pluralism. It has no single god or universally agreed upon pantheon of gods. It is so broad that scholars within and without India debate its definition and origins. It is an historic blend and evolution of beliefs and practices. So it may be more accurate to recognize what a Hindu "is" and "does" rather than what they "believe." Their actual beliefs may lie hidden and unexamined.

Most Hindus, at least until recently, would accept that there is one ultimate God and the reality of a supernatural world. Most would embrace a few common ideas like karma, reincarnation, and a pantheon of deities. But these ideas are rarely central in the minds of most Hindu students. In fact, few Hindu students truly reflect on the deeper questions of life. Rather, Hindu tradition emphasizes the value of doing your duty in life—whether as student or family member—and postponing religious reflection until later. Instead, deities are worshipped for practical assistance in everyday life or simply to follow tradition.

Recently, however, younger Hindu students are questioning many traditional views and popular Hindu practices. This is new. So today, *most Hindus hold a blend of traditional and philosophical views which are not necessarily consistent, and the younger generation is increasingly agnostic or secular.*

Modern Hinduism embraces many diverse practices, philosophies, deities, and mythologies which have evolved over centuries. Therefore, what it means to be Hindu is elusive and varies with the region, family, and individual. Just as the political borders of India encircle a diverse mixture of South Asian people groups, so too the label "Hinduism" includes a diverse mixture of South Asian religious traditions.

TIMELINE OF MAJOR
EASTERN RELIGIOUS PRACTICES
(according to generally agreed upon dates)

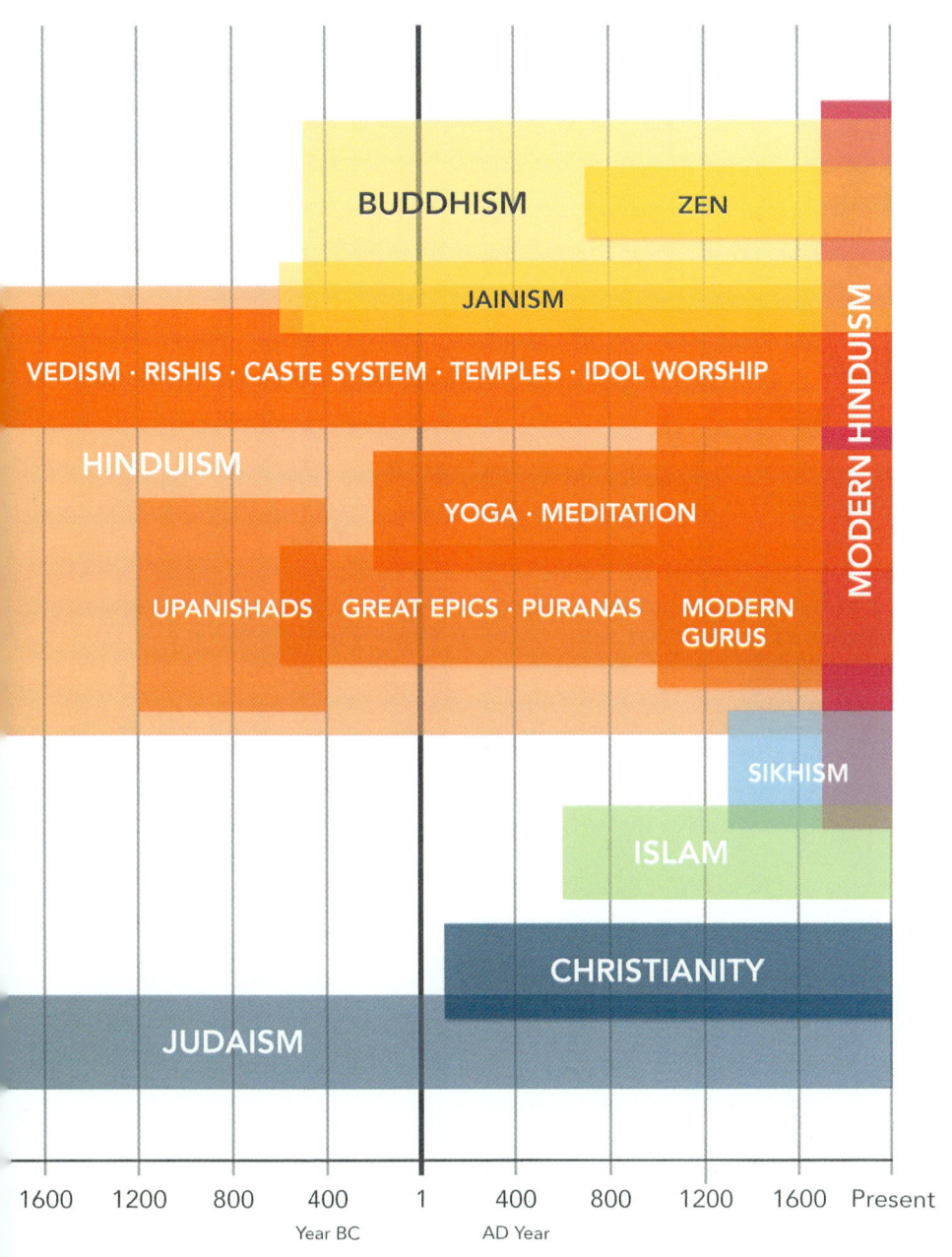

BUDDHISM

ZEN

JAINISM

VEDISM · RISHIS · CASTE SYSTEM · TEMPLES · IDOL WORSHIP

HINDUISM

MODERN HINDUISM

YOGA · MEDITATION

UPANISHADS   GREAT EPICS · PURANAS   MODERN GURUS

SIKHISM

ISLAM

CHRISTIANITY

JUDAISM

| 1600 | 1200 | 800 | 400 | 1 | 400 | 800 | 1200 | 1600 | Present |

Year BC   AD Year

▶HISTORICAL BACKGROUND

A timeline of the Hindu religious family tree shows the *antiquity, complexity, and universalizing tendency* in its tradition compared to the Abrahamic faiths.[28] Precise dating is difficult, but both Judaism and Hinduism have ancient roots. Hindu traditions blend from various sources, writings and time periods compared to the single root of biblical revelation. Note that various religious traditions (like Buddhism and Jainism) both diverged from Hindu roots and are again enveloped under the universalizing umbrella of Hinduism.

The sacred Hindu syllable, "OM"

The earliest Hindu writings (Vedas) describe hymns, prayers, and sacrifices to nature deities much like those found in the Old Testament. In fact, Indra, the most popular early deity, may be related to Zeus and Jupiter of the Greco-Roman world. These early deities are no longer worshipped. Nor are the early writings widely read. But some of these ancient traditions form the core of popular Hindu practices today. Later religious writings (notably the Upanishads from the 5th centuries BC) moved toward philosophical speculations. The sacred Hindu syllable "*OM*," which symbolizes Hinduism today, comes from this period. Its meaning varies, but there are similarities to Greek ideas of the *logos* as a power effective in the origin of the universe. These developments are foundational to the varied schools of Hindu philosophy.[29]

Eventually, traditions and mythologies of new deities (like Krishna, Ram, Shiva) grew. Some were compiled into two major epics, the *Ramayana* and *Mahabharata*, blending history and mythology like the Greek *Iliad* and *Odyssey*. Portions of these stories are the most familiar and widely-read scriptures for Hindus today. They present practical examples for a person's conduct and sacred duty in this world.

- For concise introductions to the history and beliefs of Hinduism, look at *Hinduism* by H. L. Richard or the overview in *Engaging with Hindus* by Robin Thomson.

▶ IMPACT ON HINDU STUDENTS

For simplicity's sake, it is helpful to consider two broad religious streams which impact Hindu students. These are commonly called *popular* and *philosophical* Hinduism. Most religious Hindu students will hold some elements from both.

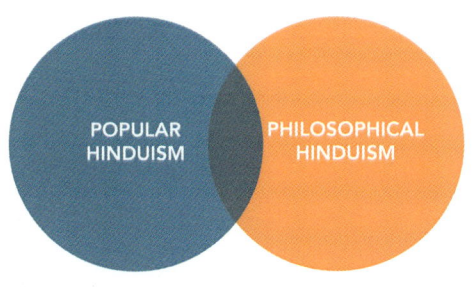

FIRST CIRCLE: POPULAR HINDUISM

The emphasis of popular Hinduism is on *rituals over beliefs*, including the worship of various deities. This stream is consistent with the early roots of Hinduism. The names have changed, but the ways of relating have not. *Popular Hinduism is the majority of Hindu religious practice.* Some common elements include:

- Offering prayers and gifts at the temple. Most prayers are ritualistic, often performed by the priest and chanted in the Sanskrit language.
- Worship (*puja*) of idols in a small shrine at home. Most families will have their own preferred deities to which they give most of their devotion in hopes that the god will help them.
- Superstitious practices which vary from region to region and family to family. Amulets are worn and rituals are performed for good luck, to ward off the evil eye, etc.
- Astrology is used by many for choosing their spouse and determining auspicious dates for weddings or other important functions.
- Devotion to a guru, which means following his or her teachings, dietary constraints, and activities (fasting, forms of yoga or meditation, etc.)

Religious charms, necklaces and bracelets are often worn by Hindu students. These are purchased from a temple or guru and worn for good luck or perhaps given as gifts by parents. A Hindu student may or may not think of them as being spiritually significant beyond reminders of family. Yet they are tangible symbols of the spiritual powers and should act as reminders of the need for intercession (Eph. 6:12).

In popular Hinduism such rituals, superstition, and temple worship are dominant. They are part of the air people breathe. Whether believed or not, they are practiced in hopes of blessings. While we were visiting a temple at a university in India, a priest remarked that visits increased during exams! Even agnostic students will perform rituals for the sake of their parents and think nothing of the inconsistency. One family had engaged the priest's services for a *puja* (worship ritual) for their daughter while she waited with boredom. So the family sometimes trumps the individual.

- Popular Hinduism represents the most common expressions of Hindu practice.

- You can freely ask South Asian friends about the practices and festivals which are most meaningful to them and why.

- Share proportionally about what is important to you in your relationship to Christ and why.

SECOND CIRCLE: PHILOSOPHICAL HINDUISM

Philosophical Hinduism seeks to comprehend ultimate reality or be united with the divine. Like the philosophers of Athens (Acts 17:18), there are diverse and sometimes contradictory schools of Hindu philosophy—both theistic and non-theistic. The most influential stream today is *advaita* (non-dualistic), popularly developed around AD 800. It says that *Atman is Brahman*—that the individual soul (*atman*) is really a part of ultimate reality or God (*Brahman*). Thus, there is no ultimate distinction between the divine and the soul. The problem is that people have forgotten that they are really a part of God and live under the illusion (*maya*) that they are separate from the divine. The goal is to realize ultimate oneness with the divine, to escape the cycle of death and rebirth (*moksha*), and to merge again with *Brahman*. The focal point is a *personal experience of realization or enlightenment. A guru or teacher is often required to lead one to enlightenment.*

Swami Vivekananda popularized his own version of *advaita* philosophy and introduced it to the West at the World Parliament of Religions in Chicago 1893. It ultimately promoted philosophy, meditation and yoga while minimizing idols and specific deities. Idols and personal deities were considered like training wheels for the ignorant. These ideas have been incorporated into much of New Age thinking and much of modern Hindu philosophy and practice today.

Not many Hindus study these philosophies. A few like to read and quote gurus. Often it is blended with traditional practice. I hear it more commonly as a defense mechanism ("All religions are the same because there is only one ultimate reality, so I don't need to consider Christ") or to soften painful issues like death ("Somehow it will all work out because in the end everything is one"). I usually avoid extended philosophical discussions since they only seem to run in circles.

- Ask what your friends think about God, origins, purpose, and what happens after death.

- Philosophical questions are okay to discuss with your South Asian friends, but *philosophical debates with those steeped in Hindu philosophy rarely lead to fruitful spiritual conversations.*

- You may share that Jesus is your guru who leads his followers into true and eternal life.

THEORY VERSUS REALITY

That is a brief description of Hinduism and its popular and philosophical streams. It may still seem exotic. But that is not the end of the matter. For all the spirituality popularized by gurus and books, Varma acknowledges that "Indians have never been, and will never be, 'other worldly'...Their spiritualism, although lofty in its metaphysics, is in religious practice mostly a means to harness divine support for power and pelf [money]. It does help, however, to weather periods of adversity."[30] So despite our religious differences, *Hindus have much in common with people everywhere.*

For most, the here and now dominates their thoughts. Ultimate questions of life after death are rarely in view. There are too many problems now to ponder distant matters of eternity or philosophy. What matters is surviving a health crisis, getting the next paycheck, or at least getting a job. In fact, even the most educated don't always question their traditions and conflicting religious views. Varma again tellingly writes:

> If technology and illiteracy coexist, so will science and superstition...Those with engineering degrees wear rings on their finger on the advice of "quacks"; they respond to matrimonial columns on the basis of caste; ...they match horoscopes and propitiate evil spirits. *What they don't ever do is question.* Tradition perpetuates itself by default, beyond scrutiny or interrogation.[31]

Therefore, one of the best things we can do with our Hindu friends is to *ask good questions that will encourage them to reflect*. As we do, they may begin to reflect more deeply.

- Ask open-ended questions such as "What do you believe God is like?" or "How did the universe and life begin?" or "What is the purpose of life?" Listen well.

- For suggestions on asking good questions, see *I Once Was Lost* by Don Everts and Doug Schaupp or *Questioning Evangelism* by Randy Newman.

THIRD CIRCLE: ATHEISM AND SECULARISM

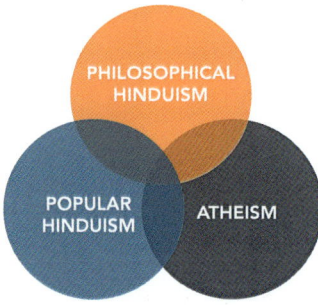

A dramatic change in the emerging generation of Hindu students is that they are questioning their beliefs and traditions *independently*. This is a hopeful trend. It means students are doing something not widely observed just a few years ago.

A 2014 Bollywood blockbuster film *PK* boldly, humorously, and irreverently challenges deep-seated religious traditions and rituals. PK is the name of an alien whose spaceship left him in India to do research. But upon landing, his radio transmitter is stolen, and he must recover it to get back home. Everyone tells him that only "God" can help him find it, which leads him on a quest among the various South Asian religions (Hinduism, Christianity, and Islam). It is particularly negative toward the financial corruption of religions in general and religious *professionals* in particular. At the same time, it questions idol worship, religious gurus, and superstition.

One memorable dialogue could almost have been lifted from the pages of Isaiah. PK purchases a small idol statue to communicate with god but then complains that it is defective when it fails to work. The shopkeeper responds heatedly that it was good quality because he made it with his own hands. With childlike innocence, PK responds incredulously, "You made god? Or god made you?" and proceeds to question the value of praying to a statue. The movie concludes that we should worship the God who created us but not the god/religions that we have made. Some Hindus were offended by the movie. Views are mixed among Hindu students. And it does not portray Christianity positively either, though it shows the distorted perceptions of it. But it shows questions about religion that more and more South Asian students are asking. *This is a momentous shift.* So the younger generation of South Asian students have a growing third circle of secularism mixed in with their religious views. These overlap often inconsistently.

- If you get a chance, watch the movie *PK* (or *OMG*). It will provide insight on how religion is viewed by many in India in this generation and the questions that students are pondering.

- Ask younger Hindus if they believe in God and what led them to that belief.

▶ FAMILY BEFORE BELIEFS

My friend Santosh illustrates this complexity of contradictory religious views, practices, and family dynamics. Soon after we first met, we connected over some shared relationship disappointments in our lives. He had to break off a relationship with a potential marriage partner who was from a caste which his family would not approve of. He chose not to go against his family's wishes. He was faithful to the vegetarian dietary restrictions of his Brahmin family. He was a natural leader and helped arrange visits to the local temple for other students and proudly posted photos there with his friends. Eventually he confided to me that he had become an atheist. He challenged family members with his questions but concluded that science was the only reliable source of truth. He purchased a new car after graduation and took me for a ride. Immediately I noticed the signs of a Hindu ritual blessing by the priest for the car. When I pointed to it and asked about it, he just smiled knowingly.

Initially, it seems hard to imagine how someone could hold together these divergent beliefs and practices. But it helps to understand that most hold to Hindu *beliefs* lightly, to religious *practices* a little more, and family *identity* tightly. Again, being a Hindu signifies more about family identity rather than Hindu religious beliefs. This helps explain again how Anand Mahadev can hold unflinchingly to his faith in Christ as the only way to God and also his family heritage as a Hindu.

Recent research by Smitha Radhakrishnan notes the importance of the family and the changes that the younger generation is bringing. She profiles the two million information technology (IT) professionals who are central to India's high-tech development and representative of the South Asian students in the U.S. These transnationals are *both influenced by their Hindu identity and simultaneously redefining Hindu identity and Indian culture.* Religiously, "the version of Hinduism that emerges is individualized yet transferable, and surprisingly uniform in its distance from ritual, its emphasis on family values, and its insistence upon the inseparability of Indianness and Hinduness."[32] The result is a more individualistic mindset which is comfortable with a cosmopolitan life but retains a commitment to the family. If this trend continues, it suggests the role of the family will remain central, but that globalism and atheism, the third circle, will grow.

RELIGIOUS DIALOGUE DOS AND DON'TS

DO	DON'T
Find out about their family and culture. What is important to them? Pray briefly with them when a need presents itself.	Don't imply that following Christ requires a rejection of their family.
Assume a belief in one supreme God—probably mysterious and unknown (Acts 17)—but note the growth of secularism.	Don't criticize Indian traditions (like caste, cows, vegetarianism, arranged marriages, etc.).
Distinguish between true and cultural Christians. Focus on the love of Christ and the gospel.	Don't argue or make religious comparisons. Let them do that and reach their own conclusions.
Assume credibility of the Bible. Freely quote it or have them read it.	Don't treat the Scriptures carelessly (like putting a Bible on the floor).
Share your testimony with humility and what God is doing in your life today.	Don't push them to a decision. Be patient and allow the Holy Spirit to convict them.

6 PRAYER AND SPIRITUAL PREPARATION

Re-read Anand Mahadev's story from chapter 1. What was the turning point in his spiritual journey? Was it a clever and polished presentation? Did someone provide apologetic answers to his questions or show how Christianity was superior? No. Instead the turning point for him was experiencing a simple prayer of a trusted friend. He writes:

> It was a simple yet delightful conversation with God that lasted all of five minutes. I don't remember it verbatim, but [my friend and his sister] articulated a prayer of blessing on my life, future, career and family. It was a simple affair—no miracles, no angels visiting. All they did was utter a deep human cry out to the creator God and his only son Jesus Christ.

Each journey of faith is unique. But Anand's experience highlights a couple of things that we should not neglect or minimize. For one, it shows the role of a trusted believer at a crucial point in his life. God brings us alongside others at different points in their spiritual journey, and we get to love them and point them to Christ. But it also shows the importance of prayer from someone with a genuine relationship with God. This was not a formal prayer but one from the heart of his friend to the heart of God. So we must not neglect the importance of prayer and our own walk with God.

▶ POWER OF PRAYER

It is hard to overstate the importance of prayer. In America, where the church is still relatively large, it is easy to rely on our own resources whether financial, numerical, or intellectual. We can learn about the centrality of prayer from our brothers and sisters where the church is small and opposition is strong. The apostle Paul encountered challenges in his ministry throughout the Greco-Roman world. He leveraged all his God-given resources (including intellectual and financial) to make Christ known. But he didn't ultimately rely on these. In Corinth, he declared:

> I was with you in weakness and in fear and much trembling, and my speech and my message were not in plausible words of wisdom, but in demonstration of the Spirit and of power, so that your faith might not rest in the wisdom of men but in the power of God. (1 Cor. 2:3-4, ESV)

In the same way, we must seek God in prayer and allow room for Hindu friends to experience the power and love of God. This could involve healing, answered prayer, sensing the love of God through believers, an experience of God in worship, or any number of other ways. Truth is vital. But heart transformation involves more than just intellectual truth. Many Hindus relate that it was the unconditional love of God that drew them to Christ.

Ajith Fernando is a thoroughly biblical scholar and author from Sri Lanka who has ministered for years among South Asian Buddhist culture. He notes the importance of both truth and power for those from non-Christian backgrounds:

> After many years of evangelistic ministry among non-Christians, I have come to the conviction that most people initially come to Christ because they have found that he can meet a need of theirs. But for them to stick with Christ long term, they must come to the conviction that he is the truth.[33]

This is not surprising, especially in fear/power cultures. A person may find Jesus beautiful and the gospel compelling. But that may not be enough. A Hindu student named Joy from South India found the Bible interesting and enjoyed the company of believers. However, she was offended at the notion that Jesus was the only way. She walked out of the room once when a speaker began sharing about the uniqueness of Christ. But when she experienced Jesus' healing power after a serious accident, that all changed and she trusted Christ. New believers from Hindu families may be fearful of abandoning their gods *entirely*, thinking, "What if my gods are angry with me, or they stop blessing me?" So we need to remember that we are not sharing a religion, an ideology, or a worldview. We are inviting them to entrust their lives to a person: the Lord Jesus who died for them and promised to forgive them and never leave nor forsake them. Let us pray boldly and expectantly for God to intervene, even miraculously, in the lives of our Hindu friends.

Let us pray boldly and expectantly for God to intervene, even miraculously, in the lives of our Hindu friends.

A 2016 article in *Christianity Today* about the growth of churches in India highlighted the need for a holistic message. A pastor said that the Indian church needs a blended ministry of word, works, and wonders. That way, the message is confirmed and consistent as it shows God's power (wonders) and confronts injustice and poverty (works), while not shying away from a clear proclamation of the gospel (word).[34]

Similarly, we long for our witness here to be authentically consistent. It should incarnate an authentic loving witness, be empowered by the Spirit, and not neglect the verbal witness of the gospel. As we reach out in authentic witness, we can pray for them and ask God to reveal himself powerfully according to their needs. As God answers, they will know that following Jesus is not superficial or Western but a deep reality of the Living Lord Jesus.

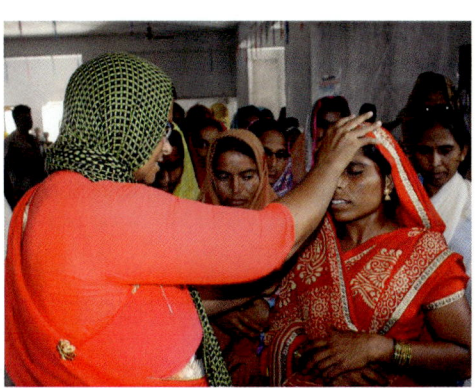

▶ PRAYING FOR SOUTH ASIAN FRIENDS

> *Lead me from falsehood to truth,*
> *Lead me from darkness to light,*
> *Lead me from death to the immortality.*
> Pavamana Mantra (approx. 6th century BC)

All people were created for God and have a God-shaped hole that only he can fill. This spiritual longing is captured in some of the well-known Hindu mantras (repeated Sanskrit prayers) like the one above. This could express a heartfelt cry for truth and life. Perhaps it will reflect the heartfelt longing as more young people are asking deeper questions about life and purpose.

Jesus met people at their point of need, whether it was the spiritual quest of Nicodemus or the loneliness of the Samaritan woman or the need for healing of the blind man. We don't know how God may choose to reveal his love and compassion. But praying for and with our Hindu friends is a powerful way we can seek to bless them. Again, Ajith Fernando allows us to see prayer in this context:

> I have never had a non-Christian refuse an offer to pray for
> him or her. Usually I do not talk much before I pray, though
> my prayer is such that one who knows very little about God

and the gospel would understand what I am saying and get to know something about the God to whom I am praying.[35]

In other words, when we pray for our Hindu friends, we aren't simply listing requests but bringing them with us into the presence of God in a way which helps them understand the person and character of God. For example, we might pray Scripture portions such as Psalm 23 or 139. We can praise God for creating us and for knowing us intimately, and we can also thank him for his goodness, fatherly love, and care. Then we humbly ask him to bless our Hindu friends and their families and bring their specific needs before him. Thus, they might taste the reality of our relationship with God and invite him to show his power. Then, when they encounter Jesus in the gospel, it will explain what they have tasted.

▶ SPIRITUAL PREPARATION

Even with the growing influence of secularism in South Asia, there remains a spiritual challenge, and Hindus often seem more open to spiritual reality than secular Westerners. It is vital for us to be spiritually prepared. The New Testament reminds us to stay alert and ready with images such as abiding in Christ, being filled with the Spirit, keeping in step with the Spirit, and putting on the armor of God. Minimally, this means that we maintain an intimate communion with the Lord (John 15:5), guard against sinful behaviors and attitudes (Gal. 5:16-26), and keep short accounts with the Lord, relying on his grace (1 John 1:9).

As we walk humbly with the Lord, we learn to rely more on the Spirit's power and leading. The book of Acts recounts the Holy Spirit's empowerment of the church as it encountered cultures of the Greco-Roman world. The Spirit gave boldness for witness, worked miracles, and at points gave specific direction for ministry.

Katie Rawson recounts a story in which God gave her insight to better communicate the gospel to a Hindu student. Sri was wrestling with a desire to trust Jesus but felt powerless to change his beliefs and thought he needed to make himself right before Jesus would accept him. She sensed the Lord giving her a picture of a cup with dirt in it and a pitcher full of clean water. She shared that picture saying that the only way to clean the cup was by allowing the pure water inside first. This illustration resonated with him, and he trusted Christ that day.[36] More than ten years later he still recalls that as his spiritual birthday and the first time he heard the gospel in a *culturally relevant way.* Hindus sometimes understand sin more as a lack of purity versus legal guilt. So this was a great picture to capture the gospel at a pivotal time. Similarly, word pictures and stories resonate well in this context. As we rely the Spirit, we can trust him to empower our words and give us insight.

Finally, a joyful and peaceful life of intimacy with Christ in a stress-filled world honors Christ and displays his power in ways that are especially appealing to Hindus. Religious pilgrims in India often seek out the peace of mind that they experience at a temple or from a special guru. The Lotus flower pictured here is a frequent symbol in many Asian religions including Hinduism, Buddhism, and Confucianism. Its precise symbolism

varies. But it commonly displays purity and serenity despite difficult circumstances. This is because the Lotus flower grows in muddy water, but the flower is always bright and clean each morning. It pictures a life that remains unstained even in an unclean world. What a wonderful image for us to embody as followers of Jesus who have the Spirit of Christ living within us (Phil. 2:14-15).

WAYS TO PRAY

Prayer guides (like pray15days.org) are available during major Hindu festivals such as Diwali, Navratri, and Holi. These encourage cultural understanding and provide insights for intercession.

7 CONSIDERATIONS FOR WITNESS

How do we bear witness to Christ in ways that are authentic, loving, and Spirit-empowered, knowing that we intersect students' lives only at certain points? We could be so paralyzed by the cultural differences that we risk nothing and share nothing. Or we could ignore the differences that exist and simply share a gospel quickly in ways that are natural to us but may unintentionally imply cultural superiority rather than the good news of Jesus' message of forgiveness to all peoples.

It is freeing to recognize that coming to faith is a process for many people. At special seasons through church history there have been moments of dramatic movements to Christ. Peter's sermon at Pentecost saw 3,000 people enter the kingdom in one day, and revival movements in church history have borne remarkable fruit in a short time. We don't want to minimize what God may do in a short period through faithful witness. Nevertheless, we don't want to assume that it must happen quickly. For those coming from a non-Christian background who are unfamiliar with the Bible, it is often a process (Acts 26:29).

Recent authors have described the stages they observed among American students' journey to faith and the roles that other believers play in that process (see *I Once Was Lost* by Don Everts and Doug Schaupp and *Cojourners* by Keith Davy). Intriguingly, similar patterns have recently been described using different language by those working among Hindu communities (including Timothy Shultz in *Disciple Making Among Hindus*). *These approaches share a remarkable similarity.*[37]

The following is an adaptation of the five thresholds (by Everts and Schaupp) for a Hindu student context, incorporating experience and insights from others. The pace and starting point will be different for each individual and will likely change with each generation of Hindu students.

THE FIVE THRESHOLDS

TRUSTING a BELIEVER		BECOMING CURIOUS		OPENING to CHANGE		SEEKING AFTER GOD		ENTERING the KINGDOM
	>		>		>		>	
Distrust to Trust		Apathy to Curiosity		Closed to Open		Meandering to Seeking		Lost to Saved

So we don't want to slavishly follow a method but prayerfully use these principles to help people move ahead in their understanding of the gospel and journey to faith.

▶ THRESHOLD 1: TRUSTING A BELIEVER

Everts and Schaupp recognize that trust is vital but distrust is the norm. If post-modern Americans with a Christian heritage have difficulty trusting believers, how much more so might it be for a Hindu who has met few genuine believers? Rather than being perceived as loving people with good news, our motives are assumed to be self-serving. Ravi Zacharias has noted that any stigma can lick a good dogma.

So a trusting relationship with an authentic believer may be a first step. This authentic witness was described earlier. Again, this is not a forced friendship or a hidden agenda. Rather it flows from genuine love (1 Cor. 16:14), hospitality to welcome strangers (Deut. 10:19), or natural connections. The key is mutual authenticity. You are open about your life, including your faith as a Christ-follower, and they are willing to relate with you knowing that.

This is an opportunity to learn about their culture, family, and religious heritage, as well as what is unique about them. You should spend more time listening and learning than witnessing. It doesn't mean you compromise your convictions or refuse to share your story of faith. But it means intentionally affirming what is good and getting to know what they personally think. You can discuss most anything freely when trust is present.

The key is mutual authenticity. You are open about your faith as a Christ-follower, and they are willing to relate with you knowing that.

In the past two decades, most Hindu students came with a high degree of distrust toward Christians. Not long ago at a national student conference, we had a track specifically for non-believing South Asian students. We invited a Hindu background believer as a guest speaker and had about a dozen Hindu students. But at our first meeting, only a couple of the students showed up and the room was tense. We later learned that these came to check out our plans while the others stayed in their room. They agreed the night before that "if they try to get us to become Christians we will just oppose them together!" But once they realized we were not there to coerce them, the tension eased and everyone else joined. We had great discussions about the gospel for the rest of the conference. A year later, one of those who had remained behind in his room placed his faith in Christ, and another brought many of his friends back the next year. Clearly, they misunderstood our motives. So sometimes, "until this framework of distrust is shifted, growth is nearly impossible."[38]

But the attitudes of younger Hindu students are changing. Suspicion and fear are still present but not nearly as much. Younger Hindu students are more at home in a global culture and seem both more skeptical and more open. In fact, many seem less fearful of spiritual dialogue. More are sharing their honest questions and curiosity about our faith. More are dropping in or willing to join Discovery Bible studies or Alpha courses. We can dialogue more quickly with those who are already asking questions. This two-way exchange is our prayer at this stage. This is an encouraging development, and we pray that it leads many to seek (Matt. 7:8).

Often, *a good indication of trust is when they invite us into their life or into deeper dialogue*. The key here is *invitation*. Not your invitation to them to come to your church or events, but their invitation to you. That is, knowing you are a genuine follower of Jesus, do they invite you deeper into their lives? If so, it is a good indication that trust barriers are breaking down. If not, you may allow the relationship to remain as it is while continuing to pray for them. But there is no need to force things further if they are not open.

- Trust is vital when mistrust and suspicion are high. Show hospitality and find ways to lovingly serve with no strings attached.

- Learn names and how to pronounce them correctly. Learn about their culture, family, and religious background, and share yours.

- Include your identity as a follower of Jesus (note that "Christian" has different connotations, so you may have to define what it means. It might help to say you were born in a Christian family but became of follower of Jesus in college or high school when you embraced the gospel).

▶ THRESHOLD 2: BECOMING CURIOUS

Trusting a believer may be a helpful step. But just because someone trusts you doesn't mean they are spiritually curious. So what does spiritual curiosity mean? It means they are curious enough to explore Jesus and faith. But it *does not* mean they are seeking God. We should not assume more spiritual interest than is present and "pour a gallon of truth into a thimble of curiosity."[39] This is especially true in South Asia where religion and spirituality are everywhere. By contrast, religion and politics are rarely discussed in America.

So how do we encourage curiosity among Hindus? Many embrace their religious traditions uncritically as their birth identity. Asking questions is a good starting point. Jesus bridged the Samaritan woman's thirst and social ostracism to eternal matters of living water by asking good questions and sharing spiritual truth proportionally. This will require patient listening to what your Hindu friends think. The goal is not to ask "gotcha" questions, correct their beliefs, or win a debate. Rather, it is to help them reflect for themselves about what they believe. At the same time, we will learn more about what they value and see many good elements in their culture and faith. Our hope is that the Holy Spirit may provoke curiosity about Jesus and we may find people of peace (Luke 10:6), those like the Samaritan woman who are open to more spiritual truth and ultimately bring others along as well (John 4:28-30).

Promoting curiosity with thoughtful, open-ended questions is not as easy as it sounds. It takes discipline for us who prefer to speak or answer questions. But it is worth the effort. Vishnu, a Hindu background believer, described how quickly he defended his Hindu beliefs when a friend began asking him questions. Even though he wasn't a committed Hindu, he staunchly argued for traditional beliefs. But even as the words came out of his mouth, he found himself wondering if he truly believed what he was defending. Vishnu began to read the Bible to prove his friend wrong. In the process, the Holy Spirit convicted him of his pride. Eventually he became of follower of Jesus and led several family members to Christ.

Stories are another natural way to encourage curiosity. Hindus are accustomed to learning spiritual truths this way. It could be a story from the Bible, a parable of Jesus, or something from your own life. Although many have studied in Catholic, English language schools, few know the basics of the gospel. They are familiar with isolated Bible stories like Adam and Eve or Noah, but they have rarely heard the stories put together. When a Hindu student attended a Bible discussion for the first time, he was surprised to learn that Moses was not God and that Christians don't pray to angels.

Share personal and practical examples of biblical truth. Religious practice in India is typically less about eternal matters and more about meeting needs of life. Religious beliefs may be compartmentalized from daily life. Students are anxious about academic success and finding a job. Share something you are learning personally of God's work in your life. Finally, the new generation of globalized and secular Hindus have a high regard for science. We can encourage curiosity by thoughtful challenges to naturalistic evolution and by pointing to a grand designer.

*They are familiar with isolated Bible stories...
but they have rarely heard the stories put together.*

An indication that your friends are spiritually curious is that they begin to initiate spiritual questions. Do they ask spiritual questions without being prompted? Do they respond with curiosity to a short parable or story from the Bible as it relates to their life? *Many Hindus hold off their real questions until they know they can trust someone with them.* When they do, most don't hesitate to ask. So this is a positive step. If not, continue to pray and see if there are any barriers. They may be fearful. Or they may be culturally curious but not spiritually curious.

- Ask thoughtful, open-ended questions which make them think.

- Share stories or parables of Jesus and practical examples of God's work in your life.

- Challenge naturalistic assumptions of secular students with evidence for a Creator such as Lee Strobel's *Case for the Creator* and Intelligent Design resources.

▶ THRESHOLD 3: OPENING TO CHANGE

The third threshold marks a turning point in a person's life but is also the most difficult. It is easier to remain passive or even curious about Christ than risk change. But why is it so difficult? Everts notes that for post-modern Americans, "questioning your own worldview and contemplating the Christian perspective for yourself is revolutionary."[40] How much more difficult must it be for a Hindu who feels they have much to lose by following Jesus? Physical dangers are rare. But there are strong cultural and spiritual pressures.

Culturally, the social and emotional stress from the family is high. Externally, there are pressures to remain committed to the religious community of their birth. Even those like Anand, who navigate these cultural pressures, struggle. They know the shame such changes might bring on their families. Internally, the implications for a person's sense of identity are challenged. Then they may wonder, "Who will I marry?" because finding a believing spouse from their own language, social, and ethnic background is difficult.

Spiritually, a devout Hindu may struggle with fears of abandoning their existing gods and religious beliefs. "Why would I risk losing the favor of the gods I worship? I wouldn't be doing so well if the gods weren't blessing me—so why take a risk?"

As you might guess, these may be less challenging for the younger generation Hindus. But even globally-minded, secular Hindus will feel the strong emotional pull of their traditions, community, and family. Becoming open to change will not be easy for them. They need to discover that Jesus is a greater treasure than anything they risk losing. It might surprise you that the hymn "I Have Decided to Follow Jesus" originates from a South Asian believer.

How can we help serve our Hindu friends who are at this point? Everts and Schaupp summarize several steps taken from Jesus' life in John 3-5. They provide some good principles and remind us not to let our own temperament dictate whether we challenge our friends to consider change. But in a South Asian context there are a couple of additional things to consider at this stage.

One is the importance of prayer as described above. Since experience is an important aspect of Hindu religion and understanding truth, it is important for us to allow room for them to experience God's power. Another help in the openness stage is meeting believers from similar backgrounds. Partnering with godly South Asian believers can be invaluable, especially at this point. Mature Hindu background believers identify with the person's struggles as they consider change. They know the issues and family pressures first hand and can offer insights and support that others cannot. When a person sees that following Jesus is viable in the lives of other Indian believers, it helps them consider the possibility for themselves. Furthermore, South Asian believers may more quickly distinguish spiritual curiosity from cultural curiosity.

Raj became curious about Jesus after observing the godly life of his Christian roommate in India. When he came to study in the U.S., he joined a Bible study group and discussed his faith questions with a believing American friend. But the turning point for him was when he met believers from Hindu families. Seeing how they followed Jesus helped him open up to change, and he soon began to follow Christ.

Ultimately, the Holy Spirit must convince hearts that following Jesus is worth it. We can lovingly walk with them in this process and challenge as appropriate, but they must choose. Let us pray with faith and ask God to display his power and love in their lives while we encourage them to "taste and see that the LORD is good" (Ps. 34:8) and to respond in faith to what they do understand (Mark 9:24).

- Prayerfully and expectantly allow room for the Holy Spirit to work and for them to experience the reality of God's presence and power.

- Introduce them to believers from similar cultural backgrounds who can help them navigate their cultural and spiritual questions.

▶ THRESHOLD 4: SEEKING AFTER GOD

The fourth threshold of seeking after God may be subtle and brief. But it is important to distinguish between true and false seekers. True seekers are not simply curious about God but are seeking Jesus specifically. They count the cost of discipleship and spend time with believers. But there are a couple of points that need clarification for those engaging Hindu students.

The first is making the gospel clear. Hindus may struggle to understand grace versus karma/works. Every religious system including Hinduism teaches that you reap what you sow. Like most of us, Hindus find God's free grace hard to understand and accept. They may also struggle to understand sin. Some may try to make themselves pure before they can follow Christ. Hindus may ask how they can be "good enough" for God. It may help to share about Christ's work on the cross with multiple biblical pictures, including our need for purification (Mark 7:20-23) and forgiveness (Luke 23:39-43).

Secondly, a "prayer of decision or surrender" may mean different things. Such a prayer might indicate honest imitation, exploration, or genuine surrender. A person might pray a prayer simply out of respect for another, especially if it is someone older or in a position of authority. This is less likely if there is ongoing dialogue. Or it might also be prayer of sincere seeking, expressing an openness for God to work in their lives. Some may not be at a point of full understanding and surrender, while others are genuinely ready to surrender their lives to Christ. We can't know and only time will tell. But we must not assume they understand all that we expect. The wind of the Spirit blows wherever he wills, so ultimately the process will remain hidden from our eyes. Our role is to share the gospel clearly and, as appropriate, challenge them to respond and follow Christ.

We also want to provide or direct them to safe places to seek. Some churches, small groups, or fellowship groups are hospitable environments and safe for Hindu seekers as they pass through this threshold. Unfortunately, this is not always the case. Suresh, a Hindu student at this stage, had opened himself up to God in prayer, left his traditions behind, and was actively seeking Christ and biblical fellowship. On one of his first visits to a Bible-believing church, the pastor made some unkind remarks about Eastern religions. Even his American friend who brought him was uncomfortable. A few weeks later the same thing happened at a different church with a different pastor. Sadly, he did not immediately return to any Bible-believing churches, and his quest was interrupted. Those pastors surely did not intend to be unkind, but that was the effect. Our focus is to lift up the gospel and the Lord Jesus Christ and not belittle other religions.

*Prayerfully and expectantly allow
room for the Holy Spirit to work*

Finding safe places to seek requires discernment. Given the cultural background and worldview of Hindus, an ideal place might be a family-sized setting in which they can worship, pray, study the Scriptures, and grow. This could be connected to a local campus fellowship, church, or home fellowship group. There is no perfect setting, but we can provide wise options.

- Show how the gospel is good news in a variety of ways—atonement and cleansing from sin, guilt, and impurity; freedom and power over sin and evil powers; removal of shame and restoration of God's honor.

- Recognize that a prayer of commitment might indicate sincere imitation, exploration, or surrender. Time will tell. Simply be careful of assumptions.

- Help find safe, hospitable settings for people to seek.

▶ THRESHOLD 5: ENTERING THE KINGDOM

Everts and Schaupp remind us that God's kingdom is like a treasure in a field or an expensive pearl (Matt. 13:44-46). "It's a thing of great joy and great cost."[41] This stage is little different from traditional evangelism which calls for decision and commitment. We don't want to rush a decision but should be appropriately urgent. The primary distinctives for Hindus are their pace and our response.

New Hindu followers of Christ should begin their walk at their own pace. It may take time for them to put away their traditional beliefs and practices, to weigh baptism, and to find ways to share with family. When Sri embraced Christ, he stopped praying to idols and moved some of his religious paraphernalia to the closet. But it was a few weeks later before he discarded them. Such things may no longer have spiritual significance but may have emotional attachment as reminders from family. Again, faith and family are intertwined. Baptism is complicated in India by associations with organizational church membership. It may at least be perceived as having legal, financial, and community implications. Emphasize the organic identification with Christ and his body in baptism and seek wise counsel.

Faith sharing with family and friends is important but should come at their pace and initiative. Encourage them to share what God has done in their life. But it must be clear to them that it is God's work in their life and their choice—not external pressure. Remember in Anand Mahadev's story he knew the transformation that Christ did in his own heart. So he was unapologetic.

Most important is our response. It is a wonderful joy to see a Hindu friend wholeheartedly embrace the Lord Jesus, and we rejoice with them. But there is a danger of publicizing it in ways that could amplify misunderstandings. This is critical, and it needs repeating in these days of social media. *We should not pass along a person's story using their name or personal details.* A new follower of Christ is unlikely to be aware of all the family and cultural challenges they will face, so consider what is best for them even if they give permission to share their good news. Let them tell their story in their own words when they are ready as Anand Mahadev did.

Take a moment to put yourself in the shoes of Hindu parents who sacrificed financially to send their son overseas to study. They love him dearly and want the best for him. They may not be religiously devout, and they may have little contact with Christians. But they do watch TV and fear that their son will be corrupted by Western Christian culture and abandon their Hindu culture and family. So they are still at the beginning of the five thresholds—distrust. If their son becomes a believer and shares his faith with them appropriately, he could dispel many of their misunderstandings. But suppose that instead of hearing about his faith from him, they hear it from a neighbor or Facebook post. Rather than helping to build trust, the opposite has happened.
It becomes more difficult for him and family tensions are heightened. I wish this was only hypothetical. Sadly, it isn't. It happens too often.

Certainly, God can bring good things from our missteps. But an understanding of the Hindu culture and a loving, patient response can minimize this challenge. Ultimately, when God changes a person's heart, it is hard to hide the transformation (Matt. 5:14).

- Allow them to respond in faith at their own pace without pressure. We can be appropriately urgent when the time is right, but their response must be their own.

- Let them share their new faith with friends and family in appropriate ways at their pace.

- Don't take this privilege and responsibility away from them by publicizing their faith online or on social media.

▶ TIMELINE

The five thresholds are not intended to be a straitjacket to keep you from lovingly sharing your faith. But they provide a framework to serve the people God has put in your life. Each person is unique, and we intersect people at different points on their spiritual journey. Some Hindus you know for a long time may not show any interest in Jesus. Others you may encounter for just a few minutes, but they may be ready to respond to the gospel. Remember that when the Samaritan woman encountered Jesus, she went from mistrust to entering the kingdom in an afternoon. I once met a Hindu student in an airport, and though I was tired, it seemed the Lord was nudging me to talk with him. He was returning to India for summer break after a lonely year. In just a 30-minute conversation we went through the first couple thresholds quickly and ended up having a meaningful discussion about faith and the gospel. So we must ultimately keep in step with the Spirit and rely on him rather than any method.

Exciting things are happening in South Asia. The church is multiplying among many people groups, among the lower castes, and in certain regions. But the gospel remains little known or understood among middle class, urban, and high-caste Hindus—the transnational Hindu population. Openness is growing, but barriers and misunderstandings still exist. Only a very small minority of South Asia's more than one billion people are true followers of Jesus. So much of this story has yet to be written.

It is said that God's guidance is directional rather than terminal. In other words, God doesn't show us all the details of our lives at the beginning but leads us by faith, step by step in the way he has for us. Perhaps that is good counsel when engaging the Hindu world. God doesn't tell us exactly how it will look in the end but leads us step by step.

We have seen that Hindu students come from a culture that is a blend of new and old, traditional and modern, religious and skeptical, individual and family. This means that we present an unchanging gospel to a people and culture which is constantly changing. Rather than prescribe a method to imitate, it seems wiser to chart a course based on the unchanging truth of Scripture, principles from South Asian culture, and ministry experience. No one can share a culturally neutral message because every church and individual is shaped by their culture. But we can do our best to minimize the transfer of cultural Christian misunderstandings.

*Discipleship in a family-sized community
...will help ground and equip new believers*

▶ PRINCIPLES AND APPROACHES

This booklet has observed diverse elements from the history, traditions, and worldview of the Hindu people and the way the younger generation is changing. We've seen that religion and culture are often closely tied to South Asian identity. Evangelists and Christian ministries are often suspected as being culturally, financially, or politically motivated. We've also noted the strong family identity around which South Asian culture is tied. The family exerts a strong gravitational pull on individual decisions, even among the younger generation. In fact, family is probably a stronger influence on South Asian identity than is religious faith. Among transnationals and the younger generation, these traditions are loosening. Thinking is more individualized, secular, and scientific. But family identity will likely remain the center of South Asian identity. So a fruitful path forward must include consideration of *both the generational changes and the importance of family and belonging.*

There are several broad approaches to ministry with South Asian international students: programmatic, individual, contextual, and familial:

PROGRAMMATIC approaches are event-oriented and geared toward the broadest numbers. These typically include meals, cultural events, trips, Bible studies, and English learning opportunities (many Bible studies initially function as English learning opportunities). In the past, few Hindus were attracted to these events because they had little need for English learning, little interest in the Bible, and preferred culturally familiar settings. With globalization, there is more openness to these activities and desire for cross-cultural friendships. Events can be good starting points. However, the long-term impact of these approaches by themselves tends to be limited.

INDIVIDUAL approaches mean broadly sowing the gospel with everyone (or whoever comes) and seeing who responds positively. This approach has advantages. It is a simple and repeatable pattern to follow and teach, so it is reproducible. Over time, the younger generation of South Asians may respond more to individual approaches than in the past. Still, those who respond positively will need culturally appropriate follow-up. South Asians tend to be suspicious of strangers, so if there is no context or relationship, the barriers remain high. And for those with no background, an isolated gospel presentation may confuse rather than enlighten.

a Telugu translation of the Bible

HIGHLY CONTEXTUAL approaches seek to incarnate the gospel in Hindu cultural and religious forms. There is a wide spectrum of contextualized approaches. These value Hindu culture and want to plant the gospel in it without passing along Western cultural forms. This intention is good and there are positive examples of this among Hindu diaspora communities. But the knowledge required may be beyond the reach for many in the U.S. Further, the cultural specialization needed for a particular Hindu community, say in language and worship forms, may not fit the cultural variety of Hindu students. There is much to learn from contextual ministry. A great example is the music of Aradhna, which blends Eastern and Western instruments in Christ-focused, South Asian devotional music (aradhnamusic.com). But as the generations change, so do the preferred forms. If the core Hindu identity is the family community and not religious forms, then we must aim to see the gospel flourishing in a family context.

FAMILIAL approaches communicate and incarnate the gospel in a smaller, relational setting which corresponds more closely to a family. An advantage is that everyone comes from a family with its imperfections and flaws. Believers all have a spiritual family as well with its imperfections and flaws. Extensive cultural knowledge is not required, though a growing understanding is helpful. Faith and discipleship can be more easily reproduced with family and friends at home. That is, a new believer doesn't need to immediately learn how to organize an outreach event or travel long distances on a mission trip. Those are fine growing experiences. But it is pivotal for the gospel to transform their life and their relationships with family and friends and for them to live out their faith in that setting. A fruitful ministry with Hindu students will likely involve elements from multiple approaches. But the gospel must bring transformation at the heart level and then work its way from their family outward. So a family-sized small group setting is a vital place for this to happen.

Sai came from a devout Hindu family in India but became a believer studying in the U.S. through the witness of a classmate who also came from a Hindu family. He became actively involved in a small church fellowship and grew in his faith. When he went home for the first time, he knew it would be unwise to be too direct with his parents and elders about his faith in such a short visit, although they knew something was different. Instead, each night he gathered his siblings and cousins who were his age and began sharing Christ and singing songs with them. He knew that in time the gospel would ripple up to his parents, and he could share more with them. Soon several of his siblings became believers, and over time his mom became a secret believer and then was baptized. The gospel continues to bear fruit in his extended family today.

- Witness and discipleship in a family-sized community, ideally including some people from culturally similar backgrounds, will help ground and equip new believers for long-term fruitfulness.

▶ FAMILIAL CULTURAL COMPLEXITIES

It might appear that family concerns would decrease among younger Hindu students. But the reverse may be the case. It is true that Hindu students are now more global, more secular, and in some ways more individualistic. Greater numbers are visiting multi-ethnic campus fellowships and churches. If evangelism and discipleship are like two ends of a funnel, it appears that there is much greater openness at the wide (evangelism) part of the funnel. But we need to keep in mind what happens at the smaller end of the funnel of discipleship and life transformation.

Genuine life transformation will impact a person's family. It is a natural place for the gospel to flow as the stories of Lydia and the Philippian jailer in Acts 16 illustrate. And we have seen that the family remains a defining element of Hindu identity and belonging. But Hindus who follow Christ face many complex issues including baptism, marriage, and festival participation. The family is often the place where pressures are most intense: it is the narrow end of the discipleship funnel. That is where fruitfulness is formed.

Hindu students may appear carefree while they are completing their studies, but the question of marriage will not be far from their minds. Some adopt Western styles of dating. Others are willing to accept an arranged marriage from their parents. Some secretly engage in pre-marital relationships with their painful consequences. But when it is time for marriage, the *family's gravitational pull is strong, and even after marriage it can draw people back to familiar cultural patterns*. Unless gospel transformation reaches the heart, a new believer may quit following Christ when family pressure increases.

Marriage can become a crucible of identity for those who choose to follow Christ. Priya embraced the gospel, was baptized, and was excited about

her faith. Unfortunately, news of her baptism was spread through social media within days and created barriers with her friends and family. Shortly after graduation, she moved and accepted an arranged marriage to a Hindu guy who did not show interest in her faith. Afterwards, it seems she quit following Christ. Of course, only God knows a person's heart. We don't know all that happened. But this pattern is not unusual. By contrast, Sai in the story above married another believer from a Hindu family. Together, they are faithfully bearing fruit in their own family and reaching out to others.

For a Hindu who chooses to follow Christ from the heart, marriage will likely be a defining issue in their fruitfulness. But it is also a difficult issue of contextualization. Simple advice like "just marry a Christian" does not automatically translate in a South Asian context. For one, "Christianity" is just as culturally defined as Hinduism. Secondly, marriage is an alliance of families and not the choice of two individuals. If the families do not understand or approve of their child's faith, the issue becomes complex, involving different communities, languages, castes, and religions. Some Hindu followers of Jesus choose to marry believers from Christian families or other cultural communities. These too can be spiritually fruitful. But they should recognize the cultural complexities involved and seek to honor and serve their respective families without compromising their faith. Discipleship in a family-sized community with godly counsel from Hindu background believers will help in the journey of faith and fruitfulness. Ideally, discipleship is not a path for a new Hindu believer to walk alone.

- There are some complex family-related issues for Hindu followers of Jesus including identity, baptism, marriage, and attending religious festivals.

- Be slow to give quick answers or simple advice. Help find biblical, culturally-informed counsel.

- Marriage is often a turning point for those who are just spiritually curious or superficially following Christ. Always keep long-term faithfulness in mind.

- Marriage is complicated for believers from Hindu families. Mature Hindu background believers can help navigate these issues.

▶ SHOULD I INVITE MY HINDU FRIEND TO CHURCH?

A common question for those who engage with Hindus is whether to invite their friends to church. Answers vary. Some are so committed to a pure, contextualized Hindu background church that they discourage bringing Hindus to a Western church. They want the gospel to grow naturally and

organically among Hindu families. This desire is admirable. Indeed, we often miss the cultural forms that are unconsciously communicated in church services. They are perfectly acceptable, but they are neither biblical nor unbiblical (things such as buildings, instruments, pulpits, offerings, pews, coat and ties, or jeans and flip flops.). Religious forms reproduced in South Asia over the past few centuries reinforce the stereotype that Christianity is a Western religion. Even more

damaging than cultural forms are unwise or unkind words that create barriers to the gospel.

It is also a challenge for new believers from tight-knit Hindu families to connect deeply and grow in a culturally unfamiliar church environment. Robin Thomson describes this, noting that many "first-generation followers of Christ often find themselves caught between their family, which neither understands nor accepts their decision, and the church, which does not always seem to understand either."[42] New Hindu believers can feel isolated and lack close relationships in many churches. The challenges are real.

But it may not be possible or desirable to isolate Hindu students from Western style churches. For one, it would be difficult given the overlap of global cultures and friend groups. Younger Hindu students are more curious about other cultures. Many Western cultural forms (like instruments) are now less foreign and more popular. God has also called the local church to be his witness and we don't want to minimize that privilege.

So how do we proceed? The Church is the family of God. But, it is full of broken people like us who sometimes say the erroneous things. Misunderstandings occur. Thankfully, love covers a multitude of cultural mistakes. Yet that doesn't mean that every church is automatically the best place to bring your Hindu friends. Some are better than others at culturally sensitive hospitality. Some come closer to embodying a spiritual family than others. We in the West may learn more about biblical community as God adds brothers and sisters from the Hindu world to our communities.

So feel free to invite your Hindu friends to visit church if they are open. Religious festivals are attended by those of different faiths in India. Hindus may visit a church on Christmas and a Muslim shrine for a special holy day while regularly visiting their own preferred temples. Spiritually significant holidays like Christmas and Easter are appropriate occasions for them to see Christian worship, even for those with minimal curiosity.

But a better question is *what environment will be the best place for my Hindu friend to hear the gospel, encounter Christ, and grow?*[43] Since family is central to South Asian identity, it would be ideal to invite Hindu friends to fellowship, worship, and learn in a home or family-sized setting. Are there small groups within your church that would be good for this? Is there a small group on campus or an investigative Bible study group where your friend would be welcomed and free to ask questions? Is there a South Asian fellowship group that meets periodically for prayer and worship in their heart culture or language?

- Holidays like Christmas and Easter are natural times to invite Hindu friends to your church, even if simply for a cultural experience. Hindus commonly attend festivals of other religions.

- If your Hindu friends are interested in regularly joining you at church, that is fine. But don't assume that a large church service is the best or only place for them to investigate Christ.

- Ask what the best environment will be for them to see the gospel lived out and to grow.

- Allow them to see a variety of church forms (traditional, modern, or home-based) so that they don't mistake one cultural expression as the only "true" church.

▶ PRINCIPLES FOR FAMILIAL SETTINGS

There is no perfect family, and there will be no perfect church or small group. But there are principles that are helpful for Hindus who want to explore what following Jesus looks like. A *family-sized* group is a natural environment for deeper community and trust to form. It is also easier to reproduce at home, among friends, in the workplace, or upon return to South Asia. A *home* is ideal because it allows others to see that faith is lived out in real life, not in theory. Biblical faith is intensely practical and involves how you love and serve others in your family and work community. Life invariably involves stress from school, work, family, and children, and those are places where we learn and model dependence on God and prayer. Hindus are rightly concerned to know that God is real and is relevant.

Prayer is a practical expression of our real-world faith. This was a turning point in Anand Mahadev's experience as he realized there was more to prayer than a recitation or hope but that it was a heart-level expression of a child to God as Father. Prayer in large settings can become formal, but in a small group or family it is easier for everyone to pray freely. Hindus may even want to begin praying with you in Jesus' name early as they explore faith. God may answer them in surprising ways.

An open environment for *questions and dialogue* is important. Hindus with suspicions are more open to an exchange of ideas at first. This doesn't mean compromising the truth but rather a willingness to listen. We want to come together on an equal footing and let the Bible be central and authoritative. As we examine the *Scriptures* together, the truth will become clear, and difficult teachings (like the exclusivity of Christ) will come from Jesus and the Bible and not from us. Finally, South Asian culture is a corporate culture, and *group decisions* are common. It may not be practical for every decision to be made as a group. But sharing decisions appropriately allows for shared ownership and greater participation. Take steps to involve others in the process whether it is meeting with two or three people for a Discovery Bible study or organizing an activity or event.

If the family context is specifically South Asian, it will naturally adopt more familiar South Asian cultural elements. For example, the group nature of decisions, the family dynamics, food preferences, and the general tone of the group can be more familiar. Elements of this are hard to define because some aspects of culture are just known and experienced intuitively. It might be the sense of smell in the air from food and spices, the sense of hospitality and welcome, the sense and flow of time, or even the sense of humor. Perhaps it is a sense of familiarity and reminder of home. A new Hindu background believer joined a retreat with other believers from South Asian and Hindu families. When he returned to campus he kept saying, "they were all *so* South Asian; they had all the typical cultural habits of  my people…but they love Jesus!!" In turn, it is often these hard to define cultural elements that make a formal Western church setting feel foreign. Neither is right or wrong. But there are times when a culturally familiar family setting helps.

A South Asian family context will ideally involve a team which includes South Asian believers with a heart and vision to open their home, apartment, or dorm room. It might take on different forms, depending on the needs of the group. If the community is primarily from one language group, then it would be appropriate to relate in that culture and language. But with a transnational South Asian community, it is probably best to aim for a diverse mixture of backgrounds with English or a shared language. That way, it preserves the general South Asian cultural tone without being dominated by any one regional group. That can be a challenge if most believers come from one language group. If the leaders share a common heart to reach out to a diverse group, they will learn together how to overcome this challenge.

▶ GOD'S PURPOSE IN THE SHADOW OF THE TEMPLE

One image the Bible uses to describe the purpose for the church family is that of the temple. This common South Asian image could serve as a bridge between Hindu culture and God's plan for the world.

The temple is a picture of God's intent to dwell among his people as he first did in the garden of Eden and will again in the new creation of Revelation 21-22. It begins with a physical structure—the mobile tabernacle (Exo. 40:34) and then the permanent temple in Jerusalem (2 Chron. 7). We often think of a temple as something like a church building—a place for worship. That is, as a functional space for corporate worship. Or perhaps we view a temple like a cathedral which reminds us of the grandeur of God. But that is not what a temple is. First and foremost, a temple is *a dwelling place or palace for God*. It is a place of worship *because* God *dwells* there in a special way.[44] Conceptually:

The temple was not a structure for corporate worship but a place for God to dwell in the midst of the people. It had to be maintained in holiness and purity so that God's continuing presence could be vouchsafed. The priests existed to maintain that purity and to control access.[45]

This is similar for Hindu temples. Rather than having the one temple in Jerusalem for one God, there are multitudes of gods and multitudes of temples. But the image is similar. Temples, whether a road side shrine or a mountain top structure, are palaces for a god or a special place of meeting. Worship and prayers are offered there because a god is thought to be present or more accessible in that place.

We easily miss this association with sacred places. Hindus value religious plurality and are quite content to visit Muslim shrines, Catholic cathedrals, or other holy places to seek divine favor or peace of mind. It shows the significance of holy places to them. Hindus are accustomed to finding peace and spiritual power in special places and from special people where God seems more present. We want them to experience the true presence of Jesus in us and as we gather for worship.

Temple worship was a picture of what was to come in Christ and the church. God's presence was manifested in a special way in the Holy of Holies. It could only be entered once a year, by one man, the high priest, and only through many sacrifices. But now *something greater than the temple is here* (Matt. 12:6). Jesus "tabernacled" among us (John 1:14), was torn down (John 2:19), and then became the cornerstone of a new temple (Matt. 21:42). The new temple was inaugurated by the Holy Spirit at Pentecost, and now believers from every nation are being built into God's dwelling place (Eph. 2:22), his palace. One day, this new temple will be complete and fill all of heaven and earth as we dwell together with God (Rev. 21-22). Paul writes to the new Corinthian believers who came from temple-centric cultures, asking, "Do you not know that you are God's temple and that God's Spirit dwells in you?" (1 Cor. 3:16). In a western context, this is an interesting concept. In a Hindu context, it is stunning! This leads to a final question: *will we individually and corporately embody the true holy temple where people can encounter the reality of God's presence?*

During a trip to India, our team visited a ministry in the red-light district of a Mumbai slum. It was heartbreaking to see young girls serving as prostitutes dressed in brightly colored saris and makeup—but with empty eyes. It felt dark even at noonday. We asked one of the Indian ministry workers how she coped with the despair she saw every day. Her face brightened as she smiled and said, "When I walk here, I am the temple of the Living God!"

When we invite Hindus into our lives and families and churches, is this what they will find? Do our lives reflect the purity of God's temple? (1 Cor. 6:18-19) When people meet us or visit our churches, do they encounter something of God's new temple (1 Cor. 3:16)? May it be so, whatever approach we take.

Will we individually and corporately embody the true holy temple where people can encounter the reality of God's presence?

KEY POINTS

- The unifying temple imagery in Scripture may unfold the story of the Bible from Genesis to Revelation in a more culturally familiar way for Hindus.

- Reflect on the significance and privilege that we individually and corporately are now the temple of the living God. (1 Cor. 3:16, 1 Cor. 6:19, Eph. 2:21).

- As we lovingly welcome Hindus into our lives, families, and churches, they can encounter the transforming power and presence of the Living God dwelling in and among us.

Most Hindu students know little of the Hindu scriptures and far less about the Bible. Their knowledge of Hindu traditions comes through stories, epics on TV or movies, family rituals, and festivals. Bible knowledge comes from stories they may have heard in school (most attended Catholic schools). But few understand the big picture of the Bible, its Jewish and historical background, or Jesus' death and resurrection. *Hindus know that Jesus died on a cross. Few understand why.* As we introduce them to the Bible, we can help them connect the dots and fill in the gaps.

▶ TIPS FOR BIBLE STUDY WITH HINDUS

ASK WHAT THEY BELIEVE Growing numbers of South Asian students are disillusioned with religions in general. They may retain a superficial allegiance to Hindu practices for the sake of family while rejecting it as a religion for themselves. We should be careful not to assume beliefs that aren't there. Asking if they believe in God, and why, is a good place to start. Even among faithful Hindus there is such a diversity of beliefs that responses can vary widely from person to person. Their answers will help you choose what Bible passages and topics would be most helpful to begin with.

BUILD ON SHARED CONCEPTS India is traditionally a "spiritual" environment. Religion is a normal part of life and most acknowledge the existence of one ultimate being, the divinity (or spiritual enlightenment) of Jesus and some credibility of the Bible as a spiritual book. Their definition of God differs, and they don't see the uniqueness of Jesus. But they will discover these for themselves as they read the Bible. If they have objections to a belief, they will usually ask. You don't have to answer questions they don't have.

USE STORIES AND ILLUSTRATIONS Stories are a common way that religious ideas and morals are taught in India. Therefore, this is a natural starting point—both the individual stories and the overall story of the Bible. You might begin with parables or stories of Jesus and then introduce the overarching story beginning with Genesis. You will likely find Hindus spiritually perceptive, often picking up the meaning quickly. Simple illustrations are also helpful for communicating Biblical principles.

- Parables like the Prodigal Son, which connect to practical areas of life (relationships, family, work, money, etc.), are good starting points.
- John is good for those more religiously or philosophically minded.
- Luke (or Mark) is good for those from a more modern and scientific mindset.

OPEN DIALOGUE Allow ample room for sharing and questions—not simply a monologue. Due to religious tensions and sensitivity in India, Hindu students will likely find it less threatening if they are free to share their ideas and questions. Most Hindus have uncritically accepted the traditions and rituals that they have seen. But they may have never asked the question "Do I really believe ____?" A safe environment with open dialogue allows them to air their ideas freely while hearing new ideas. We want to encourage them to think and ask questions and let the Scripture speak for itself. Also, some may hold back deeper or personal questions until after a group discussion when they are alone with you and feel free to share personally.

Stories are a common way that religious ideas and morals are taught in India. Therefore, this is a natural starting point.

The Alpha course (alpha.org) has been well received by a number of curious Hindus. Its format blends lectures with questions, and the "A" in Alpha stands for "Ask anything you want."

MAKE QUESTIONS YOUR FRIENDS Learning to ask questions effectively is a great skill to gain. Taking the time to know your friends and what they think will give you insight into what is important to them. Otherwise, we may answer questions they do not have or care about. Don't be afraid of silence. Whenever possible, let the authority be the Bible itself. Don't answer questions with your own opinions, but quote or let them read from the Bible themselves. When exploring a passage of Scripture with a mixed audience (seekers and believers), it is important to ask questions that anyone can answer. Consider using five simple questions from the Discovery Bible study method.

1. What do you like or find interesting about the story?
2. What do you not like (or find confusing or difficult)?
3. What do you learn about people from the story?
4. What do you learn about God?
5. What did you learn from the story about anything God wants you to do or not do?

SHARE AND PRAY Often what an American calls a "Bible study" South Asians will call a "prayer meeting." This suggests that Hindus see it more holistically as a spiritual meeting. Allow time for prayer and fellowship together including specific prayer concerns. Ultimately, we want our friends to encounter Christ the Lord in the Scripture, in prayer, in worship, and in the community of believers.

BUILD COMMUNITY India is not an individualistic culture even though globalization is fragmenting some elements of the family in urban society. If possible, allow for community to grow around the exploration of Scripture through prayer, worship, and even Indian food! (In India, a meal is usually served later (8-10 pm) at the *end* of a function marking its conclusion. But this may change in the college or U.S. context, and the group's schedules will dictate the timing.) Ideally, allow Indian students or families to host it in their apartments or homes.

FOCUS ON CHRIST While we don't want to begin with the most difficult questions (like hell and the exclusivity of Christ), we cannot avoid them when they arise. Sometimes the issues are too painful to discuss and we should defer them to another time. We should address them only within a context of love and compassion. Most Hindus have some idea of  the exclusive claims of Christianity and may interpret them as cultural superiority. Christianity is understood in terms of birth community, not personal faith. *Make sure Christ and not cultural Christianity is the issue.* Help them hear the exclusive claims through the lips of Jesus (like in John 4) rather than just through the evangelist. Hell is often heard as a manipulative scare tactic. Let them see God's judgment through the *expansiveness of God's sacrificial love in the death of Jesus Christ. It is for all people everywhere in every age.*

▶ FREQUENTLY ASKED QUESTIONS (FAQS) FROM HINDU STUDENTS

Growing numbers of younger Hindu international students seem both more spiritually curious and skeptical. Through surveys of South Asian students, we have discovered some common spiritual questions. This list is not exhaustive but perhaps it can provide some starting points.

1. AREN'T ALL RELIGIONS BASICALLY THE SAME, AND DON'T ALL PATHS LEAD TO GOD?

Pluralism seems virtually fundamental to the Hindu worldview. This issue is multi-faceted: influenced by Hindu scriptures,[46] religious history, politics, and the desire to maintain relational harmony. Critically, we must continually distinguish between religion and relationship. Here are some points to keep in mind:

- *"Should I address this question now?"* Is this a pressing issue or a painful reaction? Some speak of "all paths as valid" not because of personal beliefs but to preserve relational harmony in a religiously diverse region periodically marred by religious violence and sectarian tensions. Sometimes it is better to defer the question until later if it is emotionally charged.

- Christianity, as one of many "religions," is little different from other religions as it is typically observed—going to church, following rules and rituals, and trying to do good. We have no need to defend or promote Christianity as a religion. The difference is that the Lord Jesus Christ came to rescue us because we could never reach him through any religious system including Christianity. No one in any religion (including those from Christian families) can ever be *good enough* for God.

- *Ask questions* to find out what they mean. Have they ever looked deeply at different religions? What did they discover?

What do all religions have in common? What is their relationship with God like? If Jesus is just one of many ways to God, then why do they think he had to die?[47]

Sometimes a simple story or analogy can help people look at the question differently.

- Geography vs. Relationship: There may be many paths up a mountain. But how many ways are there to repair a broken relationship?[48]

- People are Different: How many friends do you have named Raj? Are they all the same?

- Different Boats: It is true that many religions teach similar morals. But suppose you were shipwrecked at sea and everyone is drowning. Many boats appear, and each one is teaching people a different way to swim. Another boat is pulling people out of the water. *Which one will you go to?*[49]

- Entry Visa: There are many ways to reach the U.S. You can come by boat or airplane or drive from Canada or Mexico. But to enter the country you must have a valid visa granted by the government. You may have a visa for another country, but that won't help. And you can't just purchase a visa—it must be granted by the government. What if it is the same with God? People try to come to God with their own religious "visas"— doing good deeds required by their religion, whether Muslim or Christian, Buddhist or Hindu. But God requires an entry visa with his own stamp of authority. God offers everyone this type of visa freely through Jesus' sacrifice and payment for us which he validated by bringing him from the death after three days never to die again.

- The Elephant and the Blind Men: The analogy only works because someone sees the whole elephant. The narrator who sees the whole elephant condemns everyone else as blind. It sounds humble, but is it? Can you see the whole elephant?[50]

Looking together at a Bible passage is helpful.

- Jesus' discussion with the Samaritan woman touches on the issue of pluralism for a cultural outsider. She asks about the right "place" of worship. The Lord Jesus tells her that true worship is in "spirit and truth," not in external rituals, and that it comes through him, the Jewish Messiah (John 4:20-26).

2. WHAT IS THE SIGNIFICANCE OF JESUS' SACRIFICE? WHY DID HE HAVE TO DIE, AND HOW DOES HIS DEATH 2,000 YEARS AGO MAKE ANY DIFFERENCE TODAY?

These questions suggest that the core issue of the gospel is not clearly understood. They likely need to understand the difference between salvation by grace versus works and relationship versus religion. Sin may be understood as something between people but not against God. Ultimately, the Holy Spirit must make the gospel clear, but we may find other ways to explain the significance of Jesus' sacrifice. Here are some illustrations and Bible passages to consider.

Forgiveness is Costly.
- *Child stealing:* Suppose a child steals something from a store and the shopkeeper chases him down the street ready to beat him. When his father sees this, he rushes to rescue his child. If the father simply says to his child, "Everything is okay. I forgive you."—the store owner will ask— "What about me and my money?" But if the father repays the shopkeeper for what was stolen, he will be satisfied and leave the child alone. So forgiveness is costly. Someone pays the price.[51]

God's Honor is Involved.
- Some Hindus might find an honor/shame explanation helpful. In the Prodigal Son parable, the father is shamed by his son's actions, but he bears the shame himself in front of his

community instead of punishing the son. For the gospel, the question is "How can God's reputation be restored because of our disobedience and failure to honor him?" Ultimately, Jesus bears the shame of our sin by dying on the cross to uphold the worth and honor of God the Father.

- The "Honor Restored" illustration freely available in the *GodTools* app, walks through the message of Jesus' death from this honor/shame perspective.

But 2,000 Years Ago?

- Through the ages, many people live in peace and security because of the sacrifices others made long before they were even born. Consider the peace in the world today because of the sacrifice of many soldiers in World War 2. Or consider the freedom many enjoy in India today because of the sacrifices of Gandhi and others for independence. Imagine how great the peace and freedom would be if the victory was won, not by the sacrifice of a man or woman, but by God himself who became a man and sacrificed his life to gain victory over sin and death.

Bible Passages

- *Luke 23:32-43* illustrates the simplicity of faith in the Lord Jesus. One thief knew his own guilt and the justice of his punishment. But he saw that Jesus was innocent and was not dying for his own karma. Somehow, he understood the significance of Jesus' death. Perhaps he saw in that moment that Jesus was paying for the sins of others. He was assured of ultimate forgiveness in that moment.
- *Hebrews* describes the purpose and fulfillment of Old Testament sacrifices. It would involve deeper study, but those from traditional backgrounds may embrace the temple, priestly, and sacrificial imagery fulfilled in Jesus Christ. (for example, Heb. 9-10)
- *John 15:13* points to Jesus' sacrifice as an expression of the *"greater love"* that he had by laying down his life for his friends. The love of the Lord Jesus Christ is put on display on the cross. *The love of God in Christ is a common theme for Hindus who trust in Christ.*

3. WHAT IS THE DIFFERENCE BETWEEN CATHOLICS AND PROTESTANTS? WHY ARE THERE SO MANY DIFFERENT TYPES OF CHURCHES?

There are several ways to answer this. You can share some from church history and theology. But that is usually too much information. An analogy may be a better place to start. Remember that there is a lot of variety in church denominations around the world. Your purpose is to *lift up Christ and not put others down* and distinguish between religions and a relationship with Christ.

BOTTLED WATER Think of how many brands there are of bottled water in the store: Aquafina, Fiji, Nestle, even generic brands. The list goes on and on. Church labels (denominations) sometimes function like bottle water brands.[52] They may provide some quality control of what the church teaches. But church labels are not always helpful or accurate. As long as the water is clean and pure, does the brand really matter? But if the water is contaminated or has bacteria in it…you don't want to drink it! To be sure it is safe to drink, you check the seal of the bottle cap. Similarly, the important thing is to make sure the church teaches what the Bible teaches (Acts 17:11).

LARGE TREE (JOHN 14-17) The global Church through history is like a huge tree with many branches. Each branch is uniquely and beautifully shaped by its own culture. All true branches come from the same root which is based on the core message of the Bible of the death and resurrection of the Lord Jesus Christ (John 14:6). But some branches are healthier than others. Through history some branches abandoned the root of Jesus Christ and now have no signs of life (John 15:6). They are hollow and brittle with buildings, organizations, and traditions but with no leaves or fruit. Other branches get weighed down by unnecessary traditions which keep them from growing in a healthy manner. Others remain vitally connected to the root with branches full of leaves and fruit. Look for healthy signs of life in a church that is connected to Jesus Christ and faithfully teaches his message.

All genuine believers and churches should be vitally rooted to

Christ and to each other in love and unity. But Christians aren't perfect. Differences in culture, preferences, and secondary issues too often create divisions between churches. Some divisions are necessary in order to preserve the truth about Jesus. But too often, churches are more divided than Christ intended (John 17:20-21).

4. WHO IS JESUS, AND WHAT MAKES HIM UNIQUE? (CAN'T HE JUST BE A GOD, GURU, AVATAR, PROPHET, NOBLE MAN?)

This question has many forms and often flows from the first question about whether all religions are the same. There are some traditional responses you can find. But it may be better to simply look together at the Bible.

- "That's a good question. Have you read any of the stories in the Bible about Jesus? Why don't we read some, and then you can decide what you think?" You can begin with stories in the gospels like Jesus calming the storm and raising the dead. Ultimately, the uniqueness of Jesus stands out.

- "Lord, liar, or lunatic?" These classic responses from C. S. Lewis and adapted in Josh McDowell's *More Than a Carpenter* may be helpful.

5. WHO NEEDS GOD AND RELIGION? DOESN'T SCIENCE EXPLAIN EVERYTHING WE NEED TO KNOW?

This is an increasingly common question. It shows that Hindu students are asking important questions, and we should encourage them in their quest. But we can point out many areas that science falls short. For example:

- Share about Blaise Pascal, the famous scientist known for describing the vacuum inside us which can only be filled by an infinite God. Encourage them to seek answers to their questions *and* to ask God to reveal himself to them.

- Ask questions to prompt their thinking. "Do you think science adequately explains love, beauty, and morality?" Science can explain what makes a sunset but not why it is beautiful. Science can tell you that a kiss creates a complex biochemical reaction. Is that all it is? If so, try telling that to your husband or wife!

- There are many excellent resources for those with secular objections to the existence of God and a willingness to inquire more. These include Intelligent Design videos like *Unlocking the Mystery of Life*,[53] *Case for Christ* and *Case for a Creator* by Lee Strobel, and *Reason for God* by Tim Keller.

▶ RESOURCES

Online Resources

Aradhna Music (aradhnamusic.com)
Jesus-centered spiritual songs in South Asian style and languages with a fusion of Eastern and Western instruments. Some music videos are on YouTube, and albums are available on iTunes.

InterVarsity International Student Ministry (ism.intervarsity.org)
Hundreds of Bible studies and other resources for reaching international students

Marg Network (margnetwork.org)
Articles, resources, and training opportunities for Making Authentic Relationships (with Hindus) Grow

Mission Frontiers India issue (tiny.cc/mf-india)
The May/June 2019 issue focuses on reaching the diverse Indian peoples

Every International (everyinternational.com)
A new website with a variety of videos and training resources to equip North American believers to reach out to international students and immigrants

Unlocking the Mystery of Life (tiny.cc/utmol)
Video series that works well with scientifically-minded or agnostic viewers

Books

A Beginner's Guide to Crossing Cultures: Making Friends in a Multicultural World by Patty Lane – Shares six lenses for understanding cultural differences and provides practical resources to help you navigate multicultural environments (in print or ebook) tiny.cc/bgcc

Christian Barriers to Jesus: Conversations and Questions from the Indian Context by J. Paul Pennington – Discusses nine struggles Hindus have around Christian customs, traditions, and churches tiny.cc/cbtj

Crossing Cultures with Jesus: Sharing Good News with Sensitivity and Grace by Katie J. Rawson – A great introduction to international student ministry and cross-cultural evangelism (in print or ebook) tiny.cc/ccwj

Disciple Making Among Hindus: Making Authentic Relationships Grow by Timothy Shultz – Shares how some Hindu communities experienced and responded to Jesus with a contextualized ministry tiny.cc/dmah

Engaging with Hindus by Robin Thomson – Introduces what Hindus believe and how Christians can reach out to them (in print or ebook) tiny.cc/ewhindus

Hinduism by H. L. Richard – Concise but thorough introduction to Hindu beliefs tiny.cc/hindu-book

I Once Was Lost: What Postmodern Skeptics Taught Us About Their Path to Jesus by Don Everts and Doug Schaupp – Introduces the five thresholds to becoming a follower of Jesus (in print or ebook) tiny.cc/iowl

Jesus Storybook Bible: Every Story Whispers His Name by Sally Lloyd-Jones – A children's (but not childish) Bible enjoyed by Hindus as an introduction to the Bible story tiny.cc/jesus-sb

Jesus Through Asian Eyes – Bible studies and a 16-question apologetics booklet specifically for South Asians (in print or ebook) tiny.cc/jtai

Living Water and Indian Bowl by Dayanand Bharati – Experiential insights into ministry among Hindus in India including some failures of previous approaches tiny.cc/lwib

REFERENCES

1 INTRODUCTION

[1] www.outlookindia.com/magazine/story/i-the-convert/238770. Used by permission. Note that Anand's story is not described in its entirety here. It simply presents a one-page editorial highlighting points that he wants his majority Hindu readers to grasp. Anand Mahadev is also author of the recently published book *Grace of God and Flaws of Men* (2018) which unfolds spiritual insights from the patriarchs of Genesis with specific insights for the South Asian professional world.

[2] Shashi Tharoor, *The Elephant, the Tiger, and the Cell Phone*, New York: Arcade Publishing, 2007, p. 9.

[3] Tharoor, *Elephant*, p. 14. A thali is like a small buffet on a single plate.

[4] P. K. Varma, *Being Indian*, New Delhi: Penguin Books, 2004, p. 38.

[5] Tharoor, Elephant, p. 90.

[6] Varma, Being Indian, p. 36.

[7] Tim Shultz, *Disciple Making Among Hindus: Making Authentic Relationships Grow*, Pasadena: William Carey Library, 2016, pp. 127-134.

2 A BRIEF HISTORY OF SOUTH ASIA

[8] Sarina Singh, "History." *India*, 13th edition. London: Lonely Planet Publications, 2009, p. 38. The general timeline of South Asian history is adapted from this article pp. 38-58.

[9] Will Durant, *The Story of Civilization: Our Oriental Heritage*, New York: Simon and Schuster, 1935, Vol. 1, p. 449.

[10] Samuel Moffett, *History of Christianity in Asia*, Volume 1, Orbis Books: New York, 2003, p. 269. Moffett qualifies this by noting that the Indian church had previously established some indigenous forms and was founded independently.

[11] Moffett, *Christianity in Asia*, pp. 266-270. Early church tradition is debated. There is plausible evidence for the establishment of a church in South Asia either from the apostolic period or minimally in the first two centuries after Christ. In fact, Moffett notes that in the 13th century, Marco Polo visited the reported site of Thomas' martyrdom. (pp. 35-36).

[12] Sarina Singh, *India*, p. 53.

3 HORIZONTAL AND VERTICAL DIVERSITY

[13] www.joshuaproject.net. As of 2018, the Joshua Project listed over 2,200 people groups in India as unreached with hundreds more if the rest of South Asia is included.

[14] Patrick Johnstone and Jason Mandryk, *Operation World*, Carlisle: Gabriel Resources, 2001, p. 310.

[15] "Unlike immigrant communities from some other countries, Indians do not blend in easily in Western cultures; they learn the new rules quickly, but unlearn their cultural particularities with great difficulty." Varma, *Being Indian*, p. 201.

[16] Tim Shultz, *Disciple Making Among Hindus*, pp. 17-19.

[17] Smitha Radhakrishnan, *Appropriately Indian: Gender and Culture in a New Transnational Class*, Durham: Duke University Press, 2011, p. 8.

4 HINDU CULTURE AND WORLDVIEWS

[18] Patty Lane, *A Beginner's Guide to Crossing Cultures*, Downers Grove: InterVarsity Press, 2002, p. 18.

[19] Elements adapted from "Faith Sharing" booklet, the "Reaching South Asians" issue of *Internationals on Campus*, and other articles.

[20] Katie Rawson, *Crossing Cultures with Jesus: Sharing Good News with Sensitivity and Grace*, Downers Grove: InterVarsity Press, 2015, p. 81.

[21] Rawson, *Crossing Cultures*, p. 83.

[22] Some elements of this diagram were first introduced to me from *H-STOP Training Notes*, Christar, 2001 but are modified and simplified.

[23] Varma, *Being Indian*, pp. 142-143.

[24] Radhakrishnan, pp. 8-18. "Transnational" is the term preferred by Radhakrishnan.

[25] Rawson, *Crossing Cultures*, p. 127.

[26] Varma, *Being Indian*, pp. 142-143.

[27] Roland Muller, *Honor and Shame: Unlocking the Door*, Philadelphia: Xlibris, 2001.

5 HINDUISM AND ITS IMPACT ON STUDENTS TODAY

[28] Timeline diagram adapted and used with permission from *Yeshu Samaj: Chat, Chai and Christ*, September, 2007, p. 25.

[29] Nicol Macnicol, *Hindu Scriptures*, Everyman's Library, London: J. M. Dent and Sons, 1938.

[30] Varma, *Being Indian*, p. 7.

[31] Varma, *Being Indian*, p. 142, emphasis mine.
[32] Radhakrishnan, *Appropriately Indian*, p. 178.

6 PRAYER AND SPIRITUAL PREPARATION

[33] Ajith Fernando, *Jesus Driven Ministry*, Wheaton, IL: Crossway Books, 2002, p. 198.
[34] Jeremy Weber, "Outpacing Persecution." *Christianity Today*, November 2016, Vol. 60, Num. 9, p 44.
[35] Fernando, *Jesus Driven Ministry*, p. 206.
[36] Rawson, *Crossing Cultures*, pp. 30-31.

7 CONSIDERATIONS FOR WITNESS

[37] In *I Once Was Lost*, Everts and Schaupp describe five thresholds which post-modern Americans passed through in their journey to faith. Another campus ministry developed the Cojourners material which sees a similar faith journey but focuses on four roles of a believer's witness (explorer, guide, builder, mentor). Intriguingly, Timothy Shultz noted a similar five-stage process in his ministry among the Hindu diaspora (relationship, experience, devotion, sacrifice, surrender). His descriptions are contextualized and some language may be challenging for a non-specialist and may not resonate with a younger South Asian generation. But the similarities and principles are noteworthy.
[38] Don Everts and Doug Schaupp, *I Once Was Lost: What Postmodern Skeptics Taught Us About Their Path to Jesus*, Downers Grove: InterVarsity Press, 2009, p. 32.
[39] Everts and Schaupp, *I Once Was Lost*, p. 62.
[40] Everts and Schaupp, *I Once Was Lost*, p. 60.
[41] Everts and Schaupp, *I Once Was Lost*, p. 106.

8 SUGGESTED APPROACHES

[42] Robin Thomson, *Engaging with Hindus: Understanding Their World; Sharing Good News*, England: The Good Book Company, 2014, p. 114.
[43] Thomson, Engaging with Hindus, pp. 105-115.
[44] In the Old Testament, the same word is sometimes used for both temple and palace. (as Heb. לְכָיֵה 'hekal' in 1 Kings 12:27; 21:1).
[45] "Temple Ideology," Ex. 25:8, *The IVP Bible Background Commentary: Old Testament*, 2000.

9 BIBLE STUDY TIPS, FAQS, AND RESOURCES

46 In the *Bhagavad Gita* Krishna says, "In any way that men love me, in that same way they find my love: for many are the paths of men, but they all in the end come to me." *Bhagavad Gita*, 4:11, translated by Juan Mascaro, London: Penguin Books, 1962.

47 Randy Newman, *Questioning Evangelism: Engaging People's Hearts the Way Jesus Did*, Grand Rapids: Kregel Publications, 2004, p. 81.

48 Dean Halverson, *The Compact Guide to World Religions*, Bethany House Publishers, 1996, p. 96.

49 Source unknown.

50 Newman, *Questioning Evangelism*, p. 69. The blind men and the elephant story originated in South Asia long ago, so there are now many variations. Typically, blind men encounter an elephant for the first time. Each man touches a different part of the elephant's body and then draws different conclusions about what the animal is like—a tree, wall, snake, or rope. The moral is that no subjective experience is the absolute truth and that no perspective (and no religion) is inherently better than any other.

51 Paraphrased from *Jesus Through Asian Eyes Booklet*, South Asian Forum of the Evangelical Alliance, The Good Book Company, 2014, Question 6.

52 I heard the first part of this analogy from a South Asian pastor (J. G.) in a talk many years ago.

53 illustramedia.com